## 28 SIMPLE ART PROJECTS FOR CHIC DÉCOR ON THE CHEAP
with 15 Full-Size, Tear-Out Templates

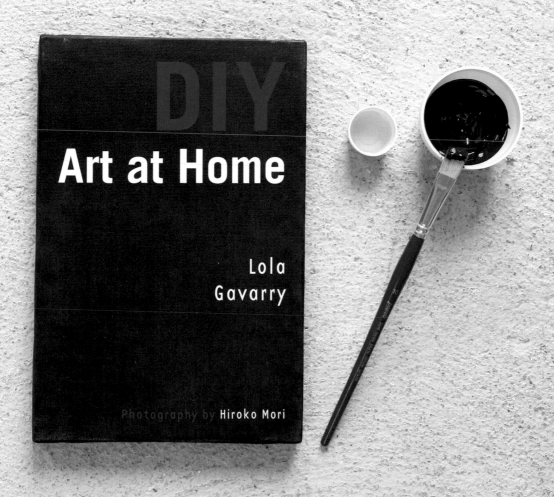

DIY

# Art at Home

Lola
Gavarry

Photography by Hiroko Mori

Watson-Guptill Publications/New York

# introduction

*DIY Art at Home* shows how easy it is to create your own modern masterpieces using a few simple art supplies and full-size, tear-out templates that are also included. The book begins with Your Home Studio, which outlines the materials and tips that you'll need to get started. The five chapters that follow offer 28 fresh, beautiful, step-by-step projects for every room, all with a clean, modern aesthetic that will complement virtually every style of decorating.

# contents

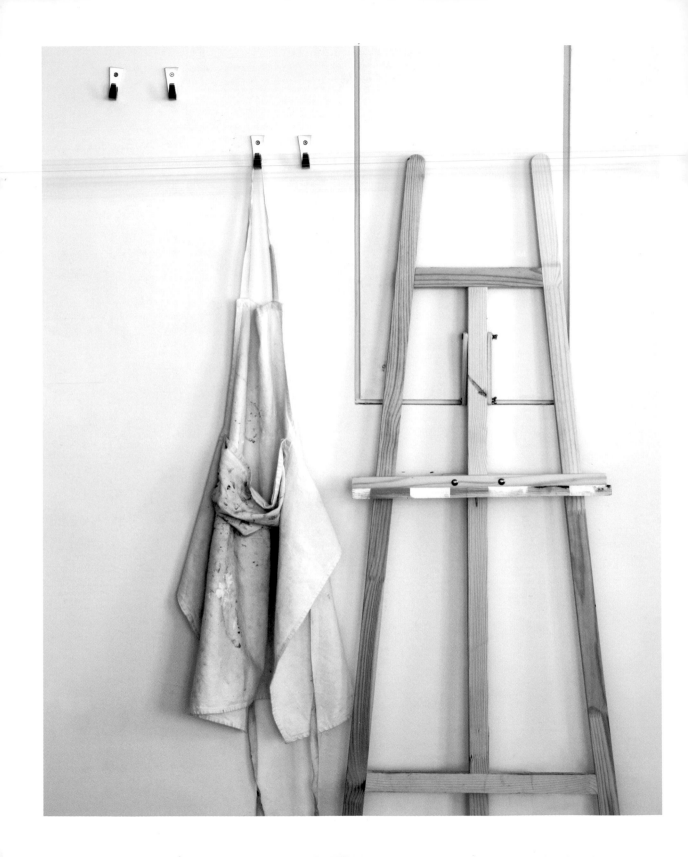

# CHAPTER 1

# YOUR HOME STUDIO

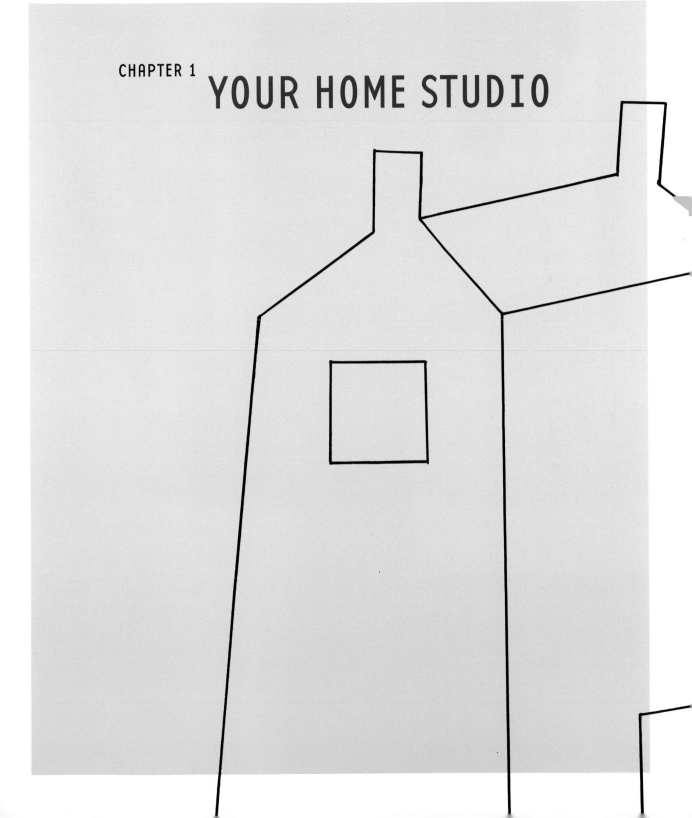

# CANVASES AND STRETCHER FRAMES

A wide range of canvases and stretcher frames are available from art stores and other suppliers of craft materials; you'll find sizes and finishes to suit every mood and style.

### Canvas Stretchers

For all of the designs in this book, we've recommended that you use white or natural-color prestretched canvas. Of course, if you already have some experience in this field and have the necessary materials, you can make your own canvas stretchers.

### Stretchers with or without Corner Braces

Whether or not your canvases are already on stretchers, you can choose either plain stretchers or ones with corner braces. The braces fit into the corners of the frame, behind the canvas. They strengthen the frame and allow you to retighten the canvas if need be.

### 3-D Stretchers

Canvas is usually stapled or nailed to the sides of the stretcher frame bars. For some of the projects in this book, we've used 3-D stretchers, where the canvas is fastened onto the back of the stretcher frame bars. These canvas stretchers do not need any additional framing. The canvas-covered sides can be painted too, and form an integral part of the design, giving the illusion of volume to the finished artwork.

**NO. 24 BRUSH** = square wash brush for large/textured areas

**NO. 18 BRUSH** = square wash brush for large/textured areas

**NO. 12 FILBERT BRUSH** = for detail work

**NO. 10 FLAT BRUSH** = for detail work

**NO. 6 ROUND BRUSH** = for detail work

**NO. 4 ROUND BRUSH** = for fine detail work

**NO. 24 BRUSH** = flat wash brush

**NO. 40 BRUSH** = for large/textured areas

**NO. 24 BRUSH** = flat wash brush

**NO. 8 ANGULAR BRUSH** = for line work

**NO. 6 SMALL BRUSH** = for delicate line work

**NO. 4 SMALL BRUSH** = for delicate line work

# BRUSHES

When choosing brushes, you'll find a wide range to select from. Depending on whether you're painting a background or the details of a design, you'll need different sizes and shapes. If you've done some painting in the past, you may already own some brushes that are sufficient; but if you're just starting out, it's easiest to buy a selection of different sizes. You can get these at most fine art and craft supply stores.

To create the art projects shown in this book, the basic size range you'll need is:

- 1 No. 18 to 24 large flat brush
- 1 No. 10 to 18 medium flat brush
- 1 No. 4 to 10 small brush (round or flat)
- Some fine brushes (pointed, flat, and angular)

## Taking Care of Your Brushes

If you take good care of your brushes, they'll last much longer. All of the projects in this book use acrylic paints, which are easy to use and to clean up.

- For water-based paints, including acrylics, clean brushes in lukewarm water using only soap. If some paint has dried on the brush, use a little Turpenoid, which is an odorless substitute for turpentine. Avoid using strong brush-cleaning products, which may damage the bristles.
- Rinse brushes thoroughly in soapy, lukewarm water. Remove excess water and leave brushes to dry with their bristles pointing upward.
- When your brushes are perfectly clean, store them flat and away from dust.

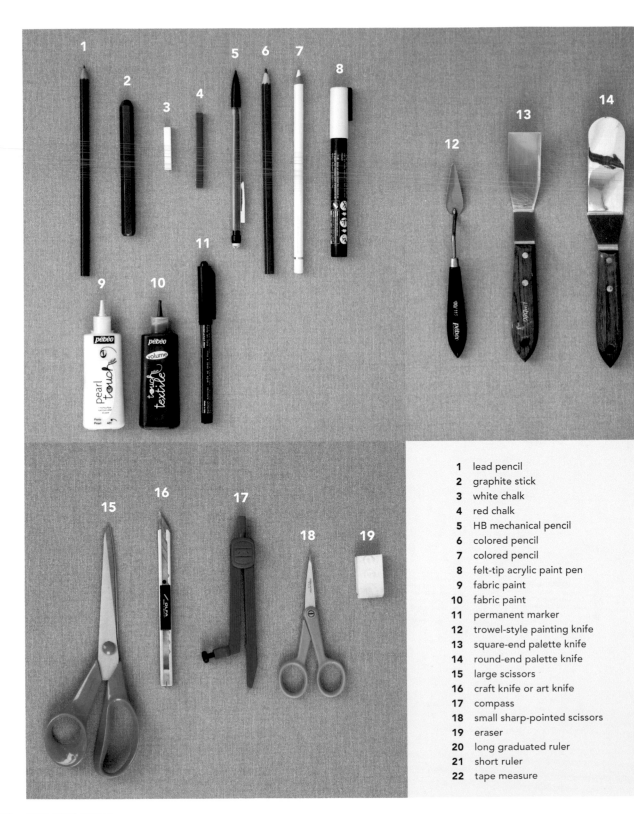

1   lead pencil
2   graphite stick
3   white chalk
4   red chalk
5   HB mechanical pencil
6   colored pencil
7   colored pencil
8   felt-tip acrylic paint pen
9   fabric paint
10  fabric paint
11  permanent marker
12  trowel-style painting knife
13  square-end palette knife
14  round-end palette knife
15  large scissors
16  craft knife or art knife
17  compass
18  small sharp-pointed scissors
19  eraser
20  long graduated ruler
21  short ruler
22  tape measure

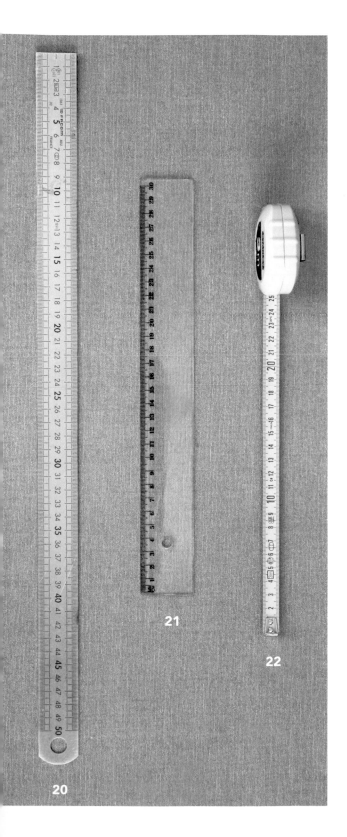

## BASIC MATERIALS

### Tools for These Four Tasks: Drawing, Applying, Cutting, and Measuring

- Lead pencil, soft lead pencil (B), mechanical pencil, graphite stick, and charcoal: For tracing or copying a motif onto a sheet of thin white paper, tracing paper, or the canvas, and for drawing directly onto the canvas.

- White chalk and red chalk: For transferring a traced motif onto a painted canvas. Use white chalk on dark backgrounds, red chalk on lighter backgrounds.

- White crayon, pastel crayon, 3-D multisurface paint, felt-tip paint pen, permanent marker, and correction pen: For very fine details, dots, and curves, which require accuracy. Use whichever you feel most comfortable with.

- Palette knives and painting knives: Palette knives are used to apply paint to large areas of the canvas. Depending on the finish you want to achieve, you can use a square-end knife for a slightly "hard" effect or a round-end knife for a smoother effect. Use trowel-shape painting knives to add small touches of paint for finer detail.

- Craft/art knife and scissors: You'll need two pairs of scissors, for different tasks. The small scissors are for precision work, as is the knife.

- Compass: Some of the projects in this book require drawing circles, which is easier with a compass. If you don't have one, saucers and small plates are good alternatives.

- Long graduated ruler, short ruler, and tape measure: Use whichever of these is most suitable for the task at hand.

1. fabric
2. colored Bristol board
3. tracing paper
4. white Bristol board
5. printed paper
6. tissue paper
7. acrylic binder
8. spray varnish
9. fixative for pencil, chalk, and charcoal
10. white adhesive
11. artist tape
12. masking tape
13. clear adhesive tape
14. spray adhesive
15. Frisket adhesive paper film

**1**

**5**

**2** **3** **4**

**6**

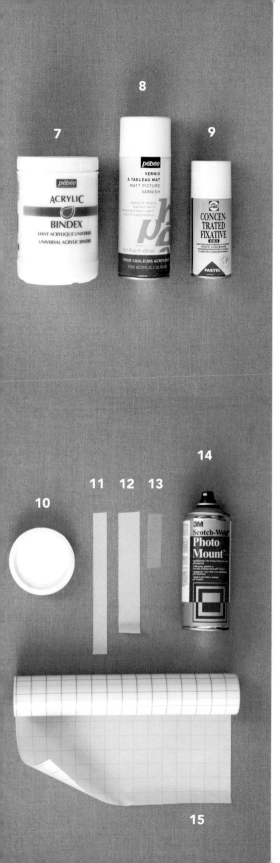

## SPECIALTY ITEMS AND TOOLS

### Everything You'll Need for Gluing, Collage, Varnishing, Coating, Fixing . . .

- Fabric: Pretty fabric isn't just for drapes and dressmaking—you'll be amazed at the possibilities for using fabrics in home décor projects. You can completely cover a canvas or panel with them, or else cut out motifs and glue them in place. Get creative with printed fabrics, mixing and matching them to unique effect. Cotton fabric is the most widely used for this purpose, but it shouldn't be so thin that the adhesive bleeds through it.

- Tracing paper, white or colored Bristol board, printed paper, and plain wrapping paper: All sorts of paper can be used for home décor projects, from tracing paper—for transferring motifs—to tissue paper and wrapping paper.

- Pencil or charcoal fixative/spray, varnish, and spray varnish: Sometimes pencil or charcoal work needs to be fixed in place, or a particularly delicate painting may need protection from dust. We'll tell you in each project which type of product to use for each task.

- Acrylic gel medium, acrylic pumice medium, modeling paste, sand mortar, and gesso paste: These help to prepare and consolidate the background of your canvas, and also to create texture. They are applied to the canvas with a palette knife before you start drawing or painting.

- Artist tape, acrylic binder, and spray adhesive: Artist tape is generally used to hold a stencil or traced motif in place, as it is easy to position and remove without damaging the surface of your project. Acrylic binder fixes materials and paper to the canvas. Spray adhesive is used for tacking photos in place.

- Frisket adhesive paper film and masking tape: For stencil work, use Frisket adhesive paper film, which are sheets of transparent adhesive film from which you can cut out shapes, as required. To mark rectangular areas that are to be painted, use masking tape.

## PAINT COLORS

### A Range of 61 Colors . . .

The artwork in this book calls for bright, strong colors; for example, the Pébéo range of 61 richly pigmented acrylic paints with a matte satin finish. They are highly resistant to fading and adhere well to the canvas.

### . . . and 1,001 Possible Variations

Although there are many colors available, we decided to create a few of our own hues for some of the projects, some of which are shown on these two pages. You'll find instructions in the projects for which base colors to use to create these unique combinations.

There's also nothing to stop you from making these projects more your own by adapting them and inventing your own shades and hues and discovering harmonious color matches.

As for paint-drying times, you should allow a minimum of 30 minutes to 1 hour for a touch-dry finish. Then, depending on the thickness of the paint and the materials used, allow 1 to 8 days for the paint to dry completely.

# PRACTICAL ADVICE

- For a background that's perfectly even in color, work with a large brush, applying the paint across the canvas in one sitting, first with horizontal and then with vertical brushstrokes (or vice versa). Using very little water, moisten the brush from time to time and then blot it before applying more paint. Let the canvas dry completely before proceeding to the next step. If you notice any variations in the background color, you can apply a second coat to eliminate them, then let dry again.

- For a graded background, use a large brush and cover the canvas using regular crossing brushstrokes from top to bottom. Work with the canvas flat to avoid the color from running down. To achieve a graded effect, add a dab of color to the white paint to start off, then add more and more white paint and water as you work down the canvas.

- For a patina-effect background, which gives a surface the uneven appearance of being aged or weathered, mix together white acrylic paint, a deeper-color acrylic paint, and two tablespoons of acrylic binder medium. Apply this mixture to the canvas with a large brush using irregular vertical strokes.

- To take good care of your paints so you can reuse them later, keep them in small glass jars with airtight lids, such as baby food or jelly jars. Always close the lids tightly when you're done painting.

- To ensure an even color when you are mixing different paints, mix them thoroughly with a brush before you start painting. Most importantly, be sure to mix enough paint for your project in advance, or you may find it difficult to re-create exactly the same shade later.

- To protect your work surface before applying a spray to the canvas, or whenever you work with the canvas flat on your work area, cover the surface with newspaper or an old sheet that you can throw out afterward. That way you don't have to worry about wiping up paint drips or getting the table sticky with sprays.

# CHAPTER 2

# LIVING ROOM CHIC

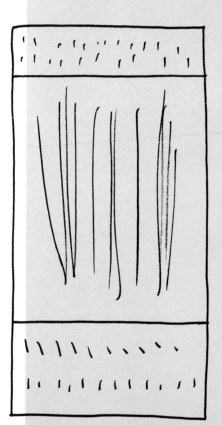

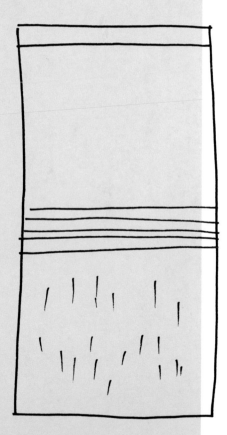

# BLUE CHECKERBOARD
Instructions on pages 26 to 29

## PETALS & LEAVES
Instructions on pages 30 to 35

# DOODLE DESIGNS
Instructions on pages 36 to 39

# VERTICAL TRIPTYCH
Instructions on pages 40 and 41

SUBTLE SHADES
Instructions on pages 42 to 45

## ZEN GARDEN
Instructions on pages 46 to 49

# BLUE CHECKERBOARD

Total time to complete: approximately 2 days
Techniques: coating / grid pattern
Pattern: Template A – 1

Finished art shown on page 20

## Other Materials

1 sheet of tracing paper, 1 sheet of white paper,
1 lead pencil, 1 stick of red chalk, 1 long graduated
ruler, scissors

## Main Materials

- 1 white canvas on 15¾" x 19⅝" (40 x 50 cm)
  stretcher frame
- 1 No. 40 large brush
- 1 No. 24 medium brush
- 1 No. 8 to 10 small flat brush
- 1 No. 4 to 6 fine brush
- Acrylic paints: indigo, turquoise blue, cobalt blue,
  ultramarine blue, cyan blue, black, titanium white,
  orange, burnt umber, cobalt violet, and crimson
- 1 artist's palette
- 1 jar of modeling paste

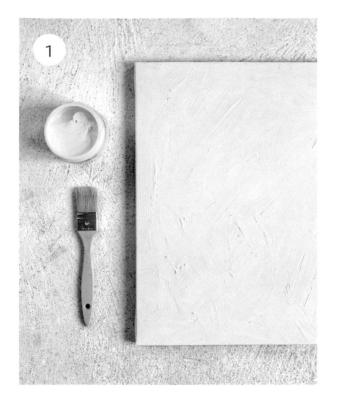

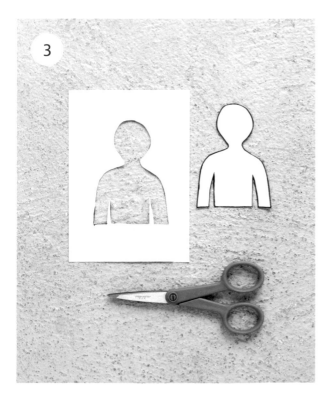

1 **Canvas Preparation: 15 minutes / Drying Time: 1 hour**
With a large brush, apply modeling paste over the entire canvas to create a textured surface. Let dry.

2 **Background: 15 minutes / Drying Time: 1 hour**
Mix cobalt violet and crimson paints and apply to the canvas with a medium brush, crossing the brush-strokes horizontally and vertically. Moisten the brush periodically using very little water and then blot it. Let the paint dry thoroughly.

3 **Tracing: 10 minutes**
Trace Pattern 1 of Template A onto the sheet of white paper, using the tracing paper and a lead pencil, then cut around the outline of the shape.

| | | | | |
|---|---|---|---|---|
| **6**<br>crimson +<br>cobalt +<br>white | **18**<br>turquoise +<br>white | **17**<br>cobalt +<br>turquoise +<br>white | **20**<br>white +<br>turquoise | **5**<br>crimson +<br>white +<br>cobalt |
| **1**<br>cobalt blue | **16**<br>**15** +<br>cobalt | **15**<br>orange +<br>white +<br>cobalt | **22**<br>turquoise +<br>white | **21**<br>turquoise +<br>orange |
| **24**<br>cyan +<br>turquoise | **23**<br>white +<br>cobalt | **4**<br>ultramarine +<br>violet | **10**<br>white +<br>crimson +<br>orange | **19**<br>white +<br>turquoise |
| **13**<br>orange | **2**<br>cobalt +<br>violet | **9**<br>white +<br>cobalt +<br>turquoise +<br>crimson | **3**<br>ultramarine +<br>indigo +<br>violet | **11**<br>white +<br>crimson +<br>orange +<br>oriental violet |
| **7**<br>white +<br>cobalt +<br>turquoise | **25**<br>turquoise | **14**<br>orange | **12**<br>**11** +<br>orange +<br>white | **8**<br>white +<br>cobalt +<br>turquoise +<br>crimson |

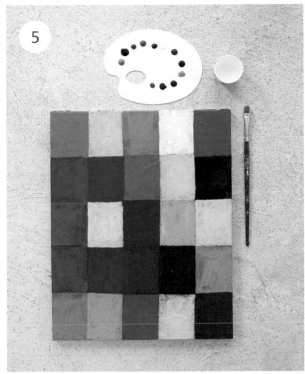

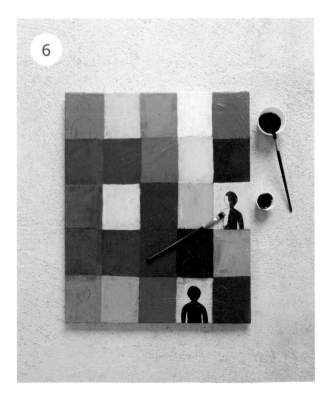

4 Grid pattern: 10 minutes

When the canvas background is dry, use the ruler to draw a grid on it with chalk. The boxes of the checkerboard should measure 3⅛" x 4" (8 x 10 cm). Place dabs of all the paints on a palette and prepare the color mixtures as shown in the color chart.

5 Painting: 2 hours / Drying Time: 2 hours

Paint the checkerboard boxes one by one, following the numbered order and using the colors listed in each box. Use several brushes to keep your work clean and neat. Allow the paint to dry thoroughly.

6 Drawing: 5 minutes / Painting: 15 minutes / Drying Time: 1 hour

When the paint is dry, trace the outline of the stenciled figure in pencil onto any selection of boxes of the checkerboard. Paint the figures black using a fine brush and a small flat brush.

# PETALS & LEAVES

Total time to complete: approximately 1 day
Technique: stenciling
Pattern: Template A – 2

Finished art shown on page 21

## Main Materials

- 1 white canvas on 11⅞" x 15¾" (30 x 40 cm) stretcher frame
- 1 No. 14 to 24 large brush
- 1 No. 8 round brush, or 1 No. 8 or 10 small flat brush
- Acrylic paints: orange and titanium white

## Other Materials

1 sheet of tracing paper, 1 piece of white Bristol board, 1 lead pencil (or 1 mechanical pencil), 1 stick of white chalk, scissors, artist tape

1 Taping: 15 minutes

Frame the edge of the canvas all the way around with artist tape, as shown, sticky side down. The tape should cover the same amount of canvas along each side so that the frame measures a uniform width on all sides. Do not fold down the outer tape edges, as you will remove the tape when the painted background is dry.

2 Background: 30 minutes / Drying Time: 1 hour

Paint the background with orange paint using the large brush, crossing your brushstrokes horizontally and vertically for an even color finish. Moisten the brush periodically using very little water and blot it before adding more paint. Let the paint dry thoroughly, and then gently remove the adhesive tape from the edge.

3 Stenciling: 15 minutes

Using the tracing paper and the lead pencil, trace Pattern 2 of Template A onto the Bristol board. Cut out the flower and remove its center.

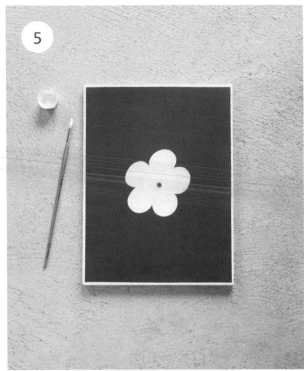

4 Drawing: 5 minutes

When the background paint is dry, place the flower stencil in the center of the canvas and trace its outline with the chalk. Mark the center of the flower with the chalk as well.

5 Painting: 15 minutes / Drying time: 10 minutes

Paint the flower white using a small brush, starting at the outer edge and filling in the rest. Be sure to leave the center of the flower orange.

6 Drawing: 10 minutes

While the paint is still wet, use the tip of the paint-brush handle (if it's fine enough) to draw the veins of the petals, or else use a mechanical pencil with no lead in it.

## ★ USEFUL TIP

For a flawless background finish with no brushstrokes showing,
apply a second and even a third coat of paint, alternating vertical
and horizontal brushstrokes. Remember to keep the brush moist
and to blot any excess water before adding more paint to it.

# SINGLE LEAF

Total time to complete: approximately 1 day
Technique: stenciling
Pattern: Template A – 3

Finished art shown on page 21

## Main Materials

- 1 white canvas on 11⅞" x 15¾" (30 x 40 cm) stretcher frame
- 1 No. 14 to 24 large brush
- 1 No. 8 round brush, or 1 No. 8 or 10 small flat brush
- Acrylic paints: green and white

## Other Materials

1 sheet of tracing paper, 1 piece of white Bristol board, 1 lead pencil, 1 stick of white chalk, scissors, artist tape

This painting is made in the same way as Petals & Leaves, using green paint for the background and Pattern 3 of Template A to trace the leaf. Draw the leaf veins on only one side of the central vein. Try to keep the taped frame dimensions consistent for all three Petals & Leaves projects.

# MULTIPLE LEAVES

Total time to complete: approximately 1 day
Technique: stenciling
Pattern: Template A – 4

Finished art shown on page 21

**Main Materials**

- 1 white canvas on 11⅞" x 15¾" (30 x 40 cm) stretcher frame
- 1 No. 14 to 24 large brush
- 1 No. 8 round brush, or 1 No. 8 or 10 small flat brush
- Acrylic paints: blue and white

**Other Materials**

1 sheet of tracing paper, 1 piece of white Bristol board, 1 lead pencil, 1 stick of white chalk, scissors, artist tape

This painting is made in the same way as Petals & Leaves and Single Leaf, using blue paint for the background and Pattern 4 of Template A to trace the nine leaves. Once again, draw the veins on only one side of the leaves and keep the taped frame dimensions consistent.

# DOODLE DESIGNS

Total time to complete: approximately 2 days
Technique: freehand

Finished art shown on page 22

## Other Materials

Artist tape, 1 soft lead pencil (B) (or 1colored pencil or 1 black fabric pen)

## Main Materials

- 9 white canvases, each measuring 4" x 4" (10 x 10 cm), on 3-D stretcher frames
- Acrylic paints: oriental violet, turquoise blue, white, black, Venice yellow, yellow earth, cadmium green, pink, silver, and orange
- Fabric paint, black
- Several No. 8 or No. 10 small flat brushes
- 1 fine brush with pointed tip
- 1 artist's palette

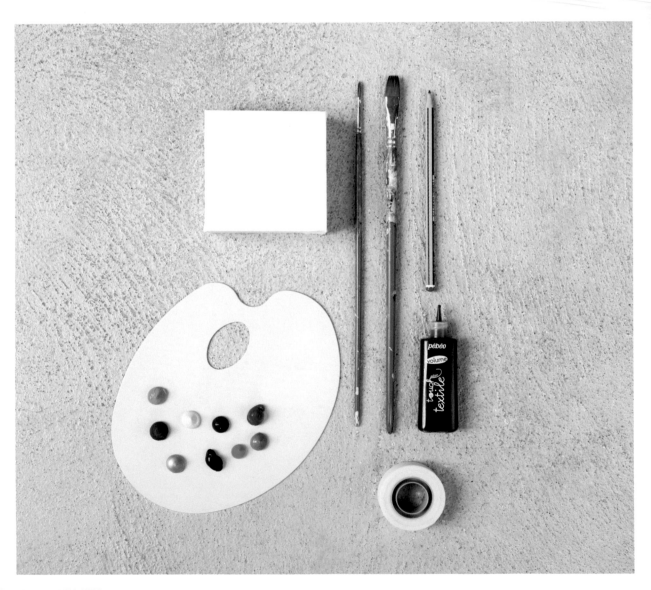

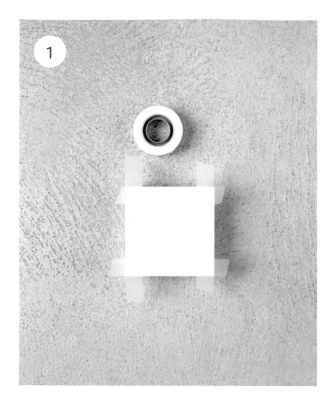

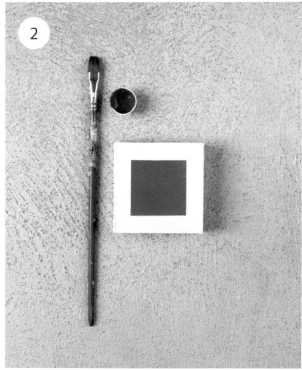

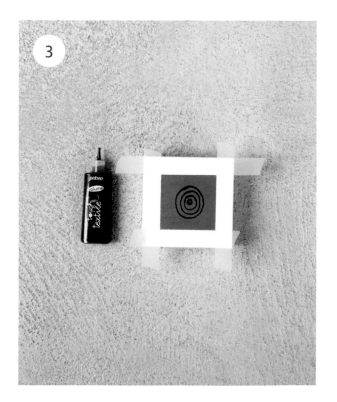

**1 Taping: 15 minutes**

Frame the edges of the canvases all the way around with artist tape, as shown, sticky side down. The tape should cover the same amount of canvas on each side so that the canvas measures a uniform width on all sides. Do not fold down the outer tape edges, as you will remove the tape when the painted background is dry.

**2 Background: 1 hour / Drying Time: 1 hour**

Paint an even background onto each canvas in various colors, applying the paint with a small brush and crossing your brushstrokes horizontally and vertically for an even color finish. Moisten the brush periodically using very little water and blot it before adding more paint. Let dry thoroughly.

**3 Motifs: 20 minutes / Drying Time: 1 hour**

When the paint is dry, draw a different doodle on each canvas using a soft lead pencil, colored pencil, or fabric paint to create spiral or dotted designs. Add touches of other colors with acrylic paint. Let dry, then gently remove the adhesive tape.

Use these ideas to inspire your own patterns and doodles.

## Colors Used

1 azo pink + black (colored pencil or fabric paint)
2 turquoise blue + black
3 Oriental violet + yellow earth
4 black + pink
5 orange + yellow earth
6 orange + black

7 cadmium green + white + black (colored pencil or felt-tip paint pen)
8 Venice yellow + yellow ochre (colored pencil)
9 silver + orange

# VERTICAL TRIPTYCH

Total time to complete: approximately 2 days

Techniques: coating / freehand

Layout Diagram: Template A – 5

Final art shown on page 23

## Materials

- 1 white canvas on 11⅞" x 23⅝" (30 x 60 cm) 3-D stretcher frame
- 1 jar of modeling paste
- 1 palette knife
- 1 painting knife
- Acrylic paints: indigo, cobalt blue, white, and Venice yellow
- 1 No. 18 to 28 large brush
- 1 fine brush

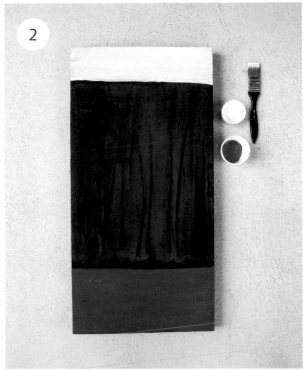

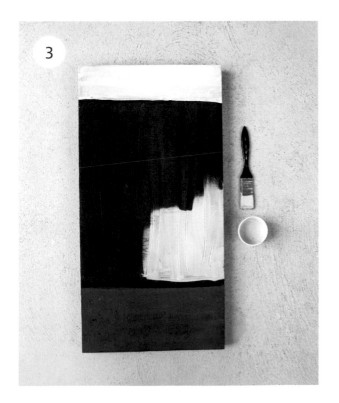

1 Coating: 30 minutes / Drying Time: overnight plus 1 hour
Using the painting knife, coat the canvas generously with modeling paste. While the paste is still wet, use the tip of the fine brush handle to draw vertical and horizontal lines and dots on the coated canvas. Let dry overnight. Then paint the background on the dry canvas in indigo with the large brush, using very little water. Let dry for 1 hour.

2 Painting: 30 minutes / Drying Time: 1 hour
When the background paint is dry, paint the upper area white and the lower area cobalt blue with the large brush, using very little water. Let dry.

3 Painting: 15 minutes / Drying Time: 1 hour
To complete the design, paint the central section of the canvas yellow with the large brush in a thin layer so that the background will show through in some places. Let dry. Now render the other two paintings the same way, using the ideas shown in Layout Diagram 5 of Template A to inspire you.

# SUBTLE SHADES

Total time to complete: approximately 2 days
Technique: freehand

Finished art shown on page 24

## Main Materials

- 8 black canvases on 7⅞" x 7⅞" (20 x 20 cm) 3-D stretcher frames
- 1 jar of modeling paste
- Acrylic paints: white, cobalt blue, and black
- 1 No. 10 to 18 medium brush

## Other Materials

1 mixing cup, 1 set of measuring spoons

1 Canvas No. 1: 20 minutes / Drying Time: 1 hour
In a mixing cup, combine some white paint, a little
blue paint, and a tablespoon of modeling paste to
make a very pale, almost white mixture. Stir the mixture well so that the color is even and then apply the
paint to the canvas with the brush, leaving a black
border around the painting. Brush the paint on at
random, leaving visible brushstrokes. Let dry.

2 Canvas No. 2: 20 minutes / Drying Time: 1 hour
Add a little blue paint to the same mixture in the
cup so that it's a shade or two darker than the first,
mix well, and apply the paint to the second canvas,
just as you did for the first painting. If necessary,
add a little more modeling paste so you get a nicely
textured finish. Let dry.

3 Canvas No. 3: 20 minutes / Drying Time: 1 hour
Add a little more blue paint to the mixture in the
cup to darken the hue, mix well, and apply the paint
to the third canvas, just as you did for the other two
paintings. Let dry.

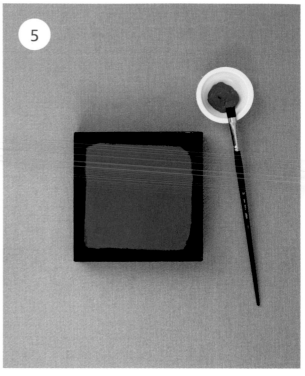

4 Canvas No. 4: 20 minutes / Drying Time: 1 hour
Add a little more blue paint to the mixture in the cup to darken it, mix well, and apply the paint to the fourth canvas, following the same procedure as you did for the previous paintings. Let dry.

5 Canvas No. 5: 20 minutes / Drying Time: 1 hour
Add more blue paint to the mixture in the cup, mix well, and apply the paint to the fifth canvas. Let dry.

6 Canvas No. 6: 20 minutes / Drying Time: 1 hour
Start with a fresh cup of cobalt blue paint and add a tablespoon of modeling paste to the cup. Mix well and apply the paint to the sixth canvas, as you did for the other paintings. Let dry.

7 Canvas No. 7: 20 minutes / Drying Time: 1 hour
  Add a little black paint to the cup, mix well, and apply the paint to the seventh canvas, as you did for the other paintings. Let dry.

8 Canvas No. 8: 20 minutes / Drying Time: 1 hour
  Add a little more black paint to the cup and mix well; the paint should be a dark blue at this point, but not black. Apply the paint to the final canvas, as you did for the other paintings. Let dry.

# ZEN GARDEN

Total time to complete: approximately 2 days
Technique: coating / freehand

Final art shown on page 25

## Other Materials

3 sheets of white paper, 1 lead pencil, scissors

## Main Materials

- 1 white canvas on 18⅛" x 21⅝" (46 x 55 cm) stretcher frame
- 1 jar of sand mortar
- 1 palette knife
- Acrylic paints: white, buff titanium/warm white, red ochre, yellow earth, and burnt sienna
- 1 No. 18 to 24 large brush
- 1 No. 10 to 18 medium brush
- 1 No. 8 or 10 small brush

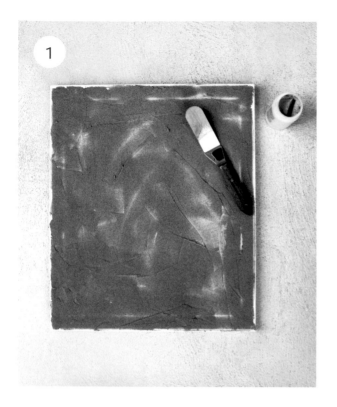

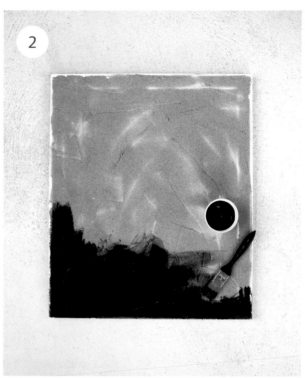

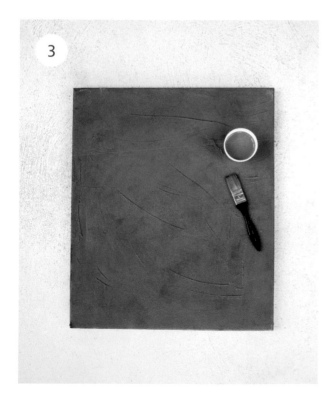

1 Background: 10 minutes / Drying Time: overnight
Use the palette knife to coat the entire surface of the canvas roughly with sand mortar. Let dry thoroughly overnight.

2 Painting: 10 minutes / Drying Time: 2 hours
Using the large brush, cover the dried mortar with a layer of red ochre paint mixed with a little water. Start at the bottom of the canvas and cross your brushstrokes. Let dry well.

3 Painting: 10 minutes / Drying Time: 2 hours
When the first layer of paint is completely dry, paint over it with a mixture of yellow earth and burnt sienna to give the color more depth and richness. Start at the bottom of the canvas and cross your brushstrokes. Moisten your brush using very little water and blotting before adding more paint. Let dry well.

4 Drawing: 20 minutes
  Using the Layout Diagram below as a guide, draw and cut out pebble shapes from the sheets of paper. Place the shapes on the canvas and trace their outlines using the lead pencil.

5 Painting: 20 minutes / Drying Time: 1 hour
  Paint the pebbles white with the medium brush, using the small brush to add highlights in buff titanium/warm white. Let dry.

## ★ PRACTICAL TIP

If you decide to paint more than one canvas using this Zen Garden motif, work on them together as a group—executing each stage at the same time for each canvas—rather than one after the other. You'll save time this way, especially for the sand mortar application; and you'll have to clean your brushes only once, at the end of each stage.

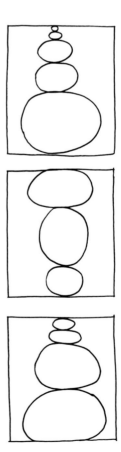

## ★ FINAL TIP

We've shown three different Zen Garden compositions on the facing
page (see finished art on page 25). You can base your design on this
layout if you want an identical "totem pole" effect, or you can create
your own composition by changing the position of the canvases when
you hang them: set them farther apart, leave spaces between them
for a "staircase" effect, or move the central canvas to one side for a
staggered effect. Or paint two identical pictures and feature them by
hanging one on either side of a piece of furniture. As you can see, this
pebble design offers any number of creative possibilities.

# CHAPTER 3

# KITCHEN INSPIRATIONS

LABEL MANIA
Instructions on pages 58 and 59

## JUICY FRUITS
Instructions on pages 60 to 63

# POP-ART DINETTE
Instructions on pages 64 and 65

## MODERN BOTANICALS
Instructions on pages 66 to 69

# HERB GARDEN
Instructions on pages 70 to 73

# SASHIKO
Instructions on pages 74 to 77

# LABEL MANIA

Total time to complete: approximately a half day

Technique: collage

Finished art shown on page 52

## Main Materials

- 1 white canvas on 11⅞" x 15¾" (30 x 40 cm) stretcher frame
- 1 jar of acrylic binder
- Acrylic paint: orange
- 1 No. 18 to 28 large brush
- Sheets of product label tissue paper of your choice

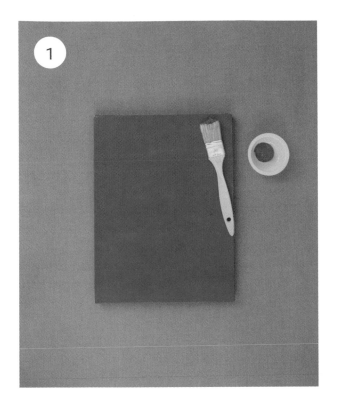

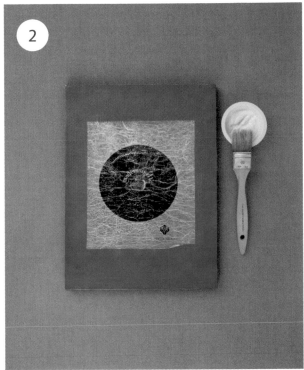

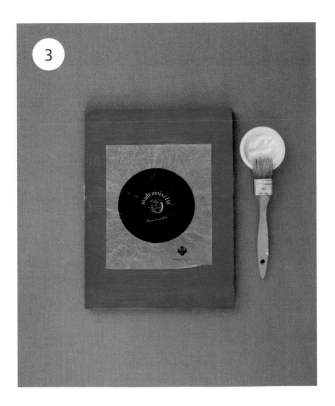

1 Painting: 30 minutes / Drying Time: 1 hour

Paint the background with the orange paint using the large brush, starting at the top of the canvas. Work with the canvas lying flat to prevent the paint from running down, and apply the paint evenly, crossing your brushstrokes horizontally and vertically over the canvas. Moisten the brush periodically using very little water and blot it before adding more paint. Let dry thoroughly.

2 Collage: 10 minutes

Smooth out the product label tissue paper carefully. Using a clean large brush, coat the center of the canvas with acrylic binder. Place the product label in the center of the glue-coated canvas.

3 Collage: 5 minutes / Drying Time: 1 hour

Using the large brush, coat the entire label sheet with acrylic binder. Let dry.

★ LITTLE TIP

Have fun painting the backgrounds in different colors and patterns (see page 52 for ideas).

# JUICY FRUITS

Total time to complete: approximately a half day
Technique: collage / stenciling
Patterns: Templates D – 1 and 2

Finished art shown on page 53

## Main Materials

- 1 white canvas on 9½" x 11⅞" (24 x 30 cm) stretcher frame
- 1 jar of acrylic binder
- Acrylic paint: cadmium red
- 1 No. 18 to 28 large brush
- 1 sheet of Frisket adhesive paper film, 9½" x 11⅞" (24 x 30 cm)

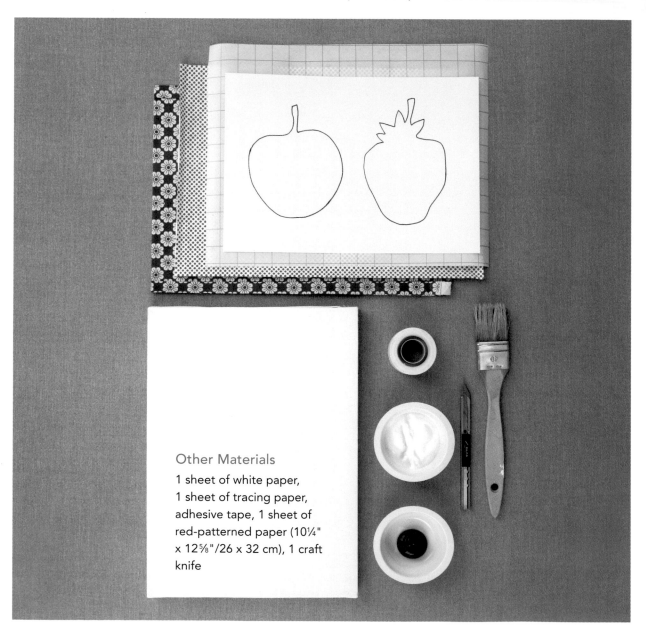

## Other Materials
1 sheet of white paper, 1 sheet of tracing paper, adhesive tape, 1 sheet of red-patterned paper (10¼" x 12⅝"/26 x 32 cm), 1 craft knife

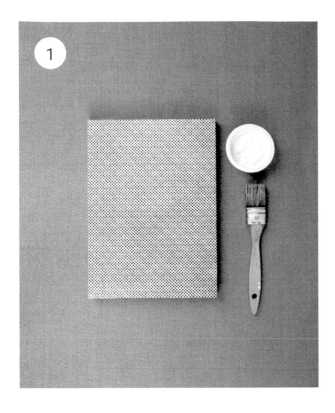

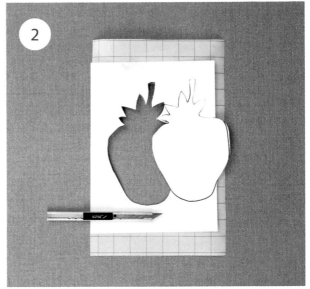

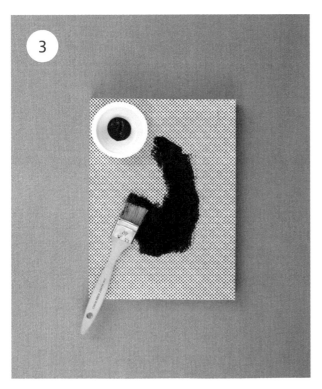

1 Collage: 30 minutes / Drying Time: 1 to 2 hours
Coat the back of the red-patterned paper with acrylic binder using the large brush. Carefully position the sheet of paper on the canvas so that it will cover all the sides evenly when folded over the edge. When it's correctly placed, smooth the paper over the canvas with the heels of your hands so that it completely adheres, with no bubbles. Carefully fold down the corners and apply a little extra glue where the corners overlap to make sure they stick cleanly. Let the glue dry.

2 Stenciling: 15 minutes
Trace Pattern 1 of Template D onto a sheet of tracing paper. Use adhesive tape to stick the drawing in the center of a sheet of Frisket film. Cut out the strawberry motif along the traced outline with the craft knife, then adhere the Frisket film stencil to the canvas, making sure to position the strawberry cutout exactly where you wish it to appear in the final painting.

3 Painting: 30 minutes / Drying Time: 1 hour
Paint over the stencil with undiluted cadmium red paint (so that the paint doesn't run under the stencil). Cross your brushstrokes horizontally and vertically for an even color finish. Let dry, then carefully remove the Frisket film stencil.

# STRAWBERRY VERSION

## ★FINAL TIP

Before you start painting the Strawberry and Apple paintings, be
sure that the stencils are perfectly centered and aligned with each
other so that you get a symmetrical finished effect when you hang
them next to each other.

# APPLE VERSION

## Main Materials

- 1 white canvas on 9½" x 11⅞" (24 x 30 cm) stretcher frame
- 1 jar of acrylic binder
- Acrylic paint: cadmium red
- 1 No. 18 to 28 large brush
- 1 sheet of Frisket adhesive paper film, 9½" x 11⅞" (24 x 30 cm)

## Other Materials

1 sheet of white paper, 1 sheet of tracing paper, adhesive tape, 1 sheet of red-patterned paper (10¼" x 12⅝"/ 26 x 32 cm), 1 craft knife

This painting is made in the same way as the Strawberry version, but use Pattern 2 of Template D to make the stencil. Choose a patterned paper that complements the one you chose for the Strawberry version background.

# POP-ART DINETTE

Total time to complete: approximately a half day
Techniques: tracing / freehand
Patterns: Templates B – 1 to 5 and C – 6 to 9

Finished art shown on page 54

## Main Materials

- 1 white canvas on 23⅝" x 35½" (60 x 90 cm) stretcher frame
- Acrylic paints: orange, cadmium green, Venice yellow, white, magenta, cyan, medium cadmium yellow, and yellow earth
- 1 No. 10 to 18 medium brush
- 1 can of fixative spray for pencil, chalk, and charcoal

## Other Materials

4 sheets of tracing paper, 4 sheets of white paper, 1 lead pencil, 1 graphite stick, scissors, masking tape

**1**

**2**

**3**

1 Painting: 30 minutes / Drying Time: 2 to 3 hours
Using the medium brush, paint patches of color on the canvas in orange, green (cadmium green and Venice yellow mixed together), pink (white and magenta mixed together), magenta, cyan, medium cadmium yellow, and yellow earth. Let dry.

2 Tracing: 30 minutes
Trace or photocopy Patterns 1 to 5 of Template B and Patterns 6 to 9 of Template C. Cut out the shapes and place them in your desired pattern over the color patches, fixing them in position with masking tape.

3 Drawing: 30 minutes / Drying Time: 1 hour
Trace the outlines of the various shapes onto the canvas using the graphite stick and then remove the pattern cutouts. Then draw in the details freehand with the graphite stick or a lead pencil. Spray the canvas with a layer of fixative spray to set the graphite. Let dry.

# MODERN BOTANICALS

Total time to complete: approximately 1 day
Technique: stenciling
Patterns: Templates D – 3 to 6

Finished art shown on page 55

## Other Materials

1 craft knife, 1 permanent marker

## Main Materials

- 1 white canvas on 18⅛" x 21⅝" (46 x 55 cm) stretcher frame
- 1 jar of gesso paste
- Acrylic paint: white, pink, cadmium green, yellow earth, cadmium red, and turquoise blue
- 1 No. 10 to 18 medium brush
- 1 No. 18 to 28 large brush
- 1 sheet of Frisket adhesive paper film, 18⅛" x 21⅝" (46 x 55 cm)

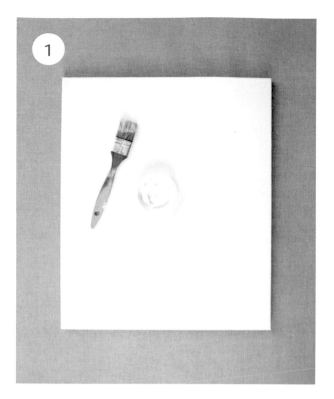

1  Coating: 20 minutes / Drying Time: 1 hour
   To protect the white background of the canvas from becoming dirty and to give it a glossy finish, coat the entire surface with gesso using the large brush. Cross your brushstrokes horizontally and vertically so that the entire canvas is covered with the gesso paste. Let dry.

2  Tracing: 30 minutes
   Using the photograph of the finished painting shown on page 55 as a guide for the layout of the final composition, use the permanent marker to trace Patterns 3 to 6 of Template D onto the sheet of Frisket film.

3  Stenciling: 30 minutes
   Adhere the sheet of Frisket film to the canvas and smooth it down to make sure there are no creases. Then use the craft knife to very carefully cut around the inside edges of the leaves, petals, and stems, removing the cut-out pieces of film to create a stencil. Press just hard enough to cut the film, but make sure you don't cut into the canvas.

**4** Painting: 30 minutes / Drying Time: 1 hour

Using undiluted paint (so that it doesn't run) and the medium brush, paint over the stencils to fill in the design, keeping the canvas flat on your work surface. Let dry. When completely dry, remove the Frisket film.

Before you start to paint, prepare the various paint mixes.

**1** Cadmium red + white = purple
**2** Cadmium green + white = soft green
**3** Yellow earth + white = light brown
**4** Turquoise blue + white = soft blue
**5** Pink + white = light pink

## ★ FINAL TIP

When you paint the flowers, start with the center. Then paint the petals, starting with the inner ones and working outward, moving around in a circle.

Another method is to paint the center of the flower first, then the upper petals followed by the lower petals.

# HERB GARDEN

Total time to complete: approximately 2 days
Technique: texture / freehand
Patterns: Template E – 2

Finished art shown on page 56

## Main Materials

- 1 natural canvas on 23⅝" x 23⅝" (60 x 60 cm) stretcher frame
- 1 tube of acrylic gel medium in red sand color
- Acrylic paint: Venice red, veronese green, green earth, vermilion, orange, cobalt blue, and ultramarine blue
- 2 No. 8 to 10 small brushes

## Other Materials

1 long graduated ruler, 1 graphite stick or lead pencil

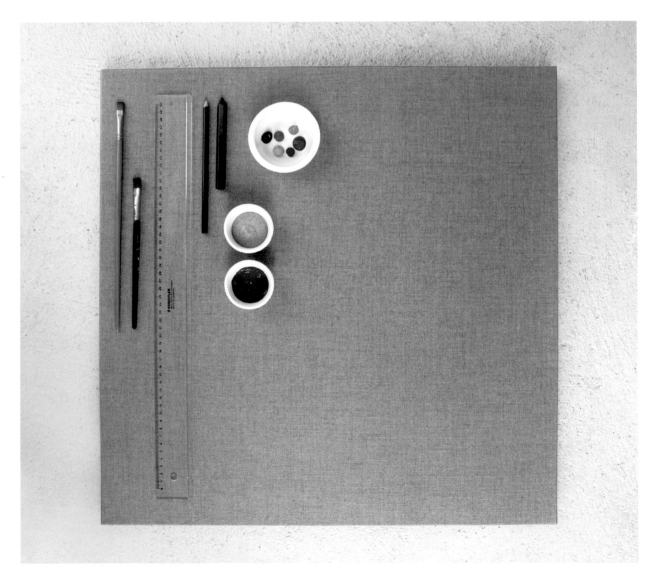

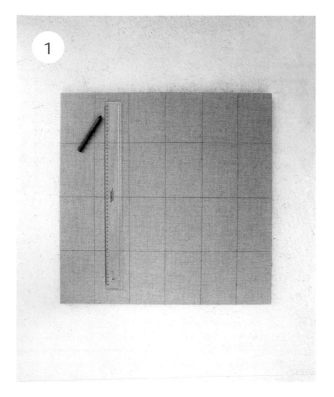

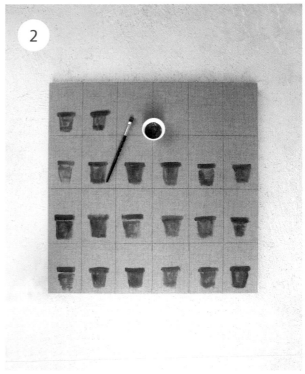

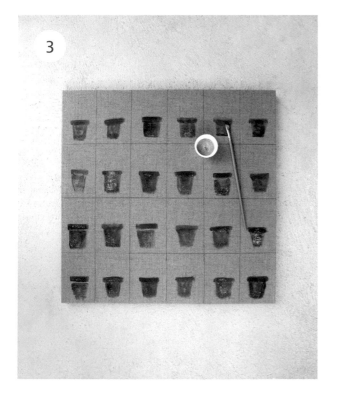

1 Grid: 20 minutes

Using the graphite stick and the ruler, draw a grid on the canvas with six columns and four rows.

2 Painting: 30 minutes / Drying Time: 1 hour

Following Pattern 2 of Template E and using Venice red paint and a small brush, paint a little flowerpot freehand in each box of the grid. Use very little water, just enough to dampen the brush before adding more paint. Let dry.

3 Texture: 30 minutes / Drying Time: 1 hour

When the paint is dry, use a clean small brush to apply the red sand acrylic gel medium over it to add texture to the flowerpots. Let dry thoroughly. Then go over each flowerpot again with Venice red paint using a small brush.

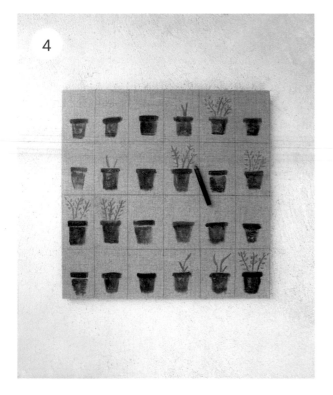

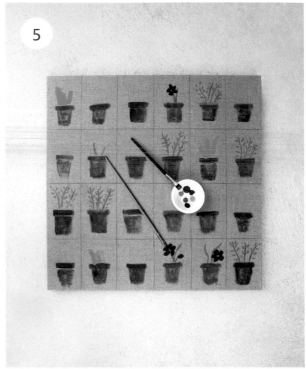

4 Drawing: 30 minutes
   Using the graphite stick, draw flower stems in some
   of the flowerpots freehand using the designs in Pattern 2 of Template E as inspiration.

5 Painting: 30 minutes / Drying Time: 1 hour
   Using the small brush, paint the leaves and flowers,
   using very little water. Let dry well.

## ★ FINAL TIP

Use the red sand acrylic gel medium generously,
applying several layers with random brushstrokes for
interesting textural effects (see details on page 72).

# SASHIKO

Total time to complete: approximately 1 day
Techniques: tracing / stippling
Patterns: Templates E – 1, F – 1 and 2, and G – 1 and 2

Finished art shown on page 57

## Main Materials

- 5 framed canvases, each 6¼" x 9½" (16 x 24 cm)
- 1 No. 12 or 14 medium brush
- Acrylic paints: ultramarine blue, cobalt blue, violet, and burnt umber
- 1 tube of white fabric paint or 1 white correcting pen, 1 white felt-tip acrylic paint pen or 1 fine round brush and 1 tube of white acrylic paint

## Other Materials

1 sheet of tracing paper, 1 lead pencil, 1 stick of white chalk, 1 scrap of cloth, scissors, artist tape

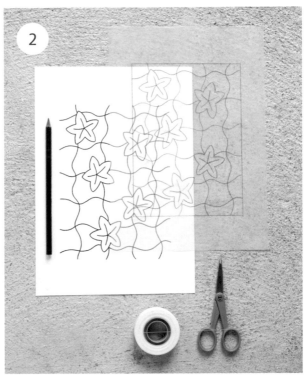

1 Background: 30 minutes / Drying Time: 1 hour
Paint the background of each canvas in the color of your choice with the medium brush, crossing the brushstrokes horizontally and vertically for an even color finish. Moisten the brush periodically using very little water and blot it before adding more paint. Let dry thoroughly.

2 Tracing: 15 minutes
Tape the tracing paper over the pattern of your choice (Templates E-1, F-1 and 2, G-1 and 2) and trace the motif with the lead pencil.

3 Chalk: 5 minutes
On the reverse side of the tracing paper, shade over the traced motif with a generous coating of white chalk, then shake the sheet of tracing paper to remove the excess chalk.

4 Drawing: 15 minutes

When the background paint on the canvas is dry, tape the sheet of tracing paper over the canvas, chalk side down. Cut the tracing paper to fit the canvas, if necessary. Using the lead pencil, retrace the outlines of the motif to transfer the chalk onto the canvas.

5 Final Motif

Remove the tracing paper and you should see a light outline of the design in chalk on the canvas.

6 Stippling: 20 minutes / Drying Time: 1 hour

Use the tube of white fabric paint (or one of the alternative materials listed) to create a stippled pattern of dots over the chalked motif, pressing very lightly on the tube. It's a good idea to practice first to learn how to make consistently sized dots. When the white motif is dry, wipe the canvas with a clean cloth to remove the chalk.

## ★ FINAL TIP

To make sure your final piece is neat and precise, it's very important that
the tracing paper not move at all when you are drawing over the outlines
of the motif. Therefore, it's best to cut the tracing paper a little smaller
than the canvas and then fix it in place securely with tape.

# CHAPTER 4

# BEDROOM INFLUENCES

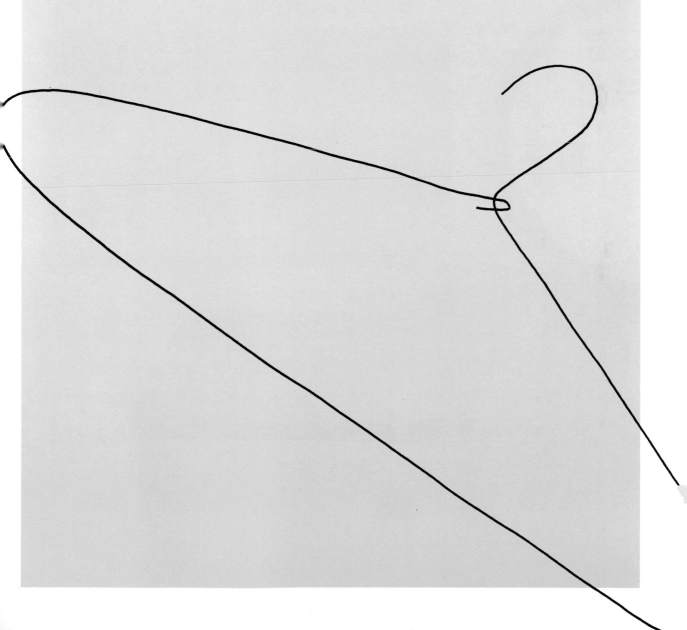

## SILHOUETTES
Instructions on pages 90 to 93

CHERRY BLOSSOMS
Instructions on pages 94 and 95

# APPAREL ART
Instructions on pages 96 and 97

## PYRAMID SCHEME
Instructions on pages 98 and 99

84

LITTLE BLUE HOUSE
Instructions on pages 100 and 101

# VACATION SKETCHBOOK

Total time to complete: approximately 2 days
Techniques: collage / tracing
Patterns: Template H – 1

Finished art shown on page 80

## Main Materials

- 2 white canvases on 9½" x 11⅞" (24 x 30 cm) stretcher frames
- 1 jar of modeling paste
- 1 jar of acrylic binder
- Acrylic paints: red ochre, burnt umber, yellow earth, cobalt blue, Hooker's green, and white
- 1 No. 10 to 18 medium brush
- 1 fine brush
- 1 can of spray varnish

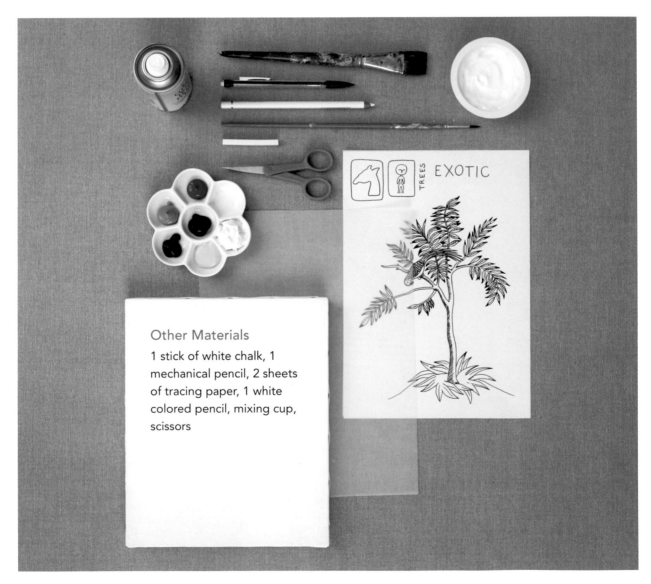

## Other Materials

1 stick of white chalk, 1 mechanical pencil, 2 sheets of tracing paper, 1 white colored pencil, mixing cup, scissors

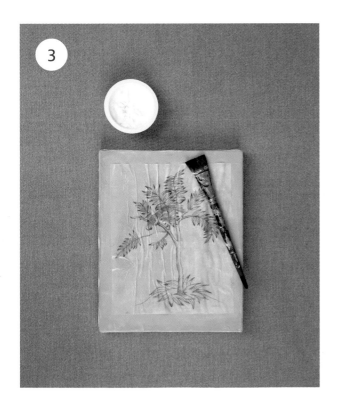

1 Background: 30 minutes / Drying Time: overnight

To create a textured background on each canvas, mix Hooker's green and white paints in a mixing cup with some modeling paste and apply the mixture generously to one canvas with the medium brush. Then mix red ochre and burnt umber paints with some modeling paste and apply the mixture to the other canvas with the clean medium brush. Let dry overnight.

2 Tracing: 30 minutes

Using the mechanical pencil, trace all of Pattern 1 of Template H onto a sheet of tracing paper and then trace the tree again on a second sheet of tracing paper. Cut out each piece of the first pattern and then coat the back of each piece generously with white chalk. Set the pieces aside.

3 Collage: 10 minutes / Drying Time: 1 hour

Using a clean medium brush, coat the green canvas with acrylic binder thoroughly. Place the second tracing of the tree on the green canvas and coat the tracing with a layer of acrylic binder. Let dry well.

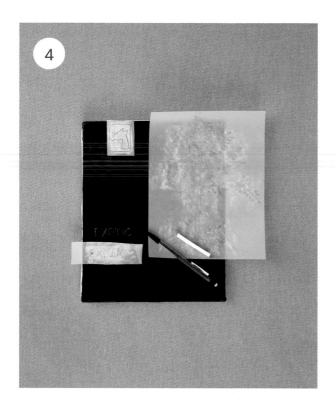

4 Drawing: 20 minutes

Place the tracing of the tree with the chalk coating onto the dark canvas, chalk side down. Trace
over the tree with a mechanical pencil so that the
chalk tracing is transferred to the canvas. Remove
the tracing paper. If necessary, trace over the motif
again with the white colored pencil if there are spots
where the chalk hasn't transferred to the canvas.

5 Painting: 30 minutes / Drying Time: 1 hour

Transfer the smaller motifs and lettering to the
canvases as explained in Step 4. Using the fine brush
and very little water, paint the backgrounds of the
inset motifs in yellow earth and the animal's head in
cobalt blue. Let dry, then apply varnish as a spray or
with a brush. Let dry thoroughly.

## ★ FINAL TIP

When applying spray varnish, place your canvas on a flat surface, hold it in place by the sides, and gently apply an even coat, making sure that the spray covers the entire surface. As you varnish your painting, take care not to leave fingerprints on the canvas, as they will show up after you have applied the varnish.

# SILHOUETTES

Total time to complete: approximately a half day
Techniques: collage / gluing / painting
Pattern: Template H – 2

Finished art shown on page 81

## Main Materials

- 1 white canvas on 6¼" x 8⅝" (16 x 22 cm) stretcher frame
- 1 piece of fabric, 14⅛" x 12⅝" (36 x 32 cm)
- Acrylic paint: black
- 1 jar of acrylic binder
- 1 No. 18 to 24 large brush
- 1 No. 8 or 10 fine round brush

## Other Materials

1 graphite stick, 1 sheet of white paper, fabric scissors

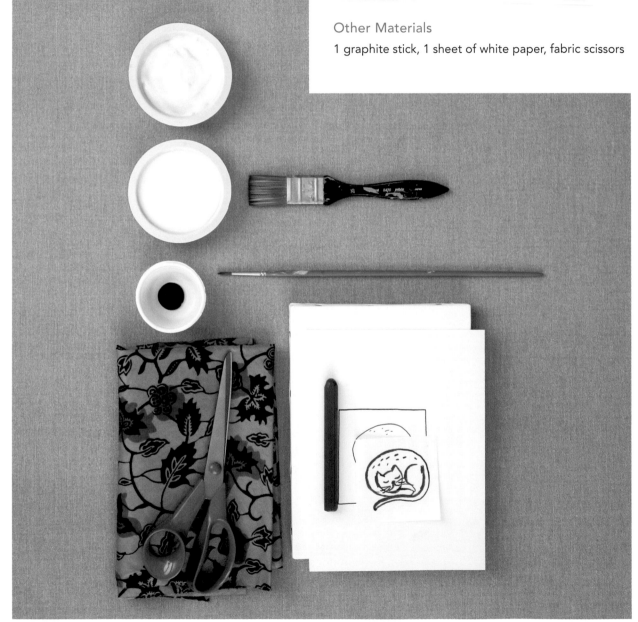

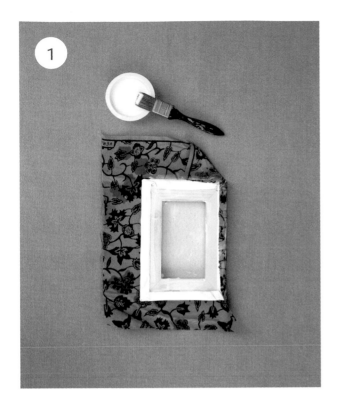

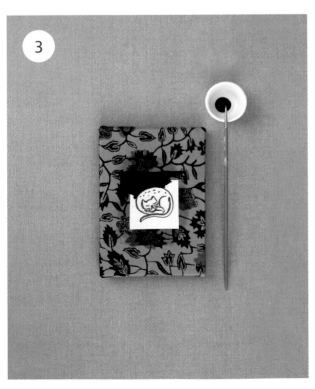

**1** Gluing: 15 minutes / Drying Time: 2 hours
Put the fabric right side down on a table and place the canvas frame on it. Fold down the four corners of the fabric into triangles and trim the fabric to form neat corners. Mark where the canvas frame aligns with the fabric corners and then remove the frame. Coat the entire surface of the fabric with acrylic binder using the large brush. Place the canvas frame back down on the fabric and firmly and carefully wrap the fabric edges around the back of the frame. Let dry.

**2** Collage: 15 minutes / Drying Time: 2 hours
Photocopy Pattern 2 of Template H and trace it onto a sheet of white paper using the graphite stick. Decide what size you want your cat drawing to be on the canvas and then cut the paper to that size in the shape of a square. Glue the drawing onto the center of the canvas using acrylic binder and the large brush. Brush a thin layer of acrylic binder over the entire canvas and the drawing. Let dry.

**3** Painting: 15 minutes / Drying Time: 1 hour
Paint the background of the drawing with black paint using the fine brush. Use very little water, just enough to moisten the brush periodically. Be careful not to let the paint bleed into the surrounding fabric. Let dry.

## ★ FINAL TIP

This picture is essentially a painted drawing glued onto fabric, which in turn is glued onto canvas, so it's essential to stretch the fabric tightly over the canvas in Step 1.

As you glue the fabric to the canvas, use the heel of your hand to firmly smooth it out to avoid creases and bubbles. Be sure to let the glue dry well before moving on to the next stage of the work.

# LE VISAGE

Total time to complete: approximately a half day
Techniques: collage / painting
Pattern: Template H - 2

## Main Materials

1 white canvas on 6¼" x 8⅝" (16 x 22 cm) stretcher frame
1 piece of fabric, 14⅛" x 12⅝" (36 x 32 cm)
Acrylic paint: white
1 jar of acrylic binder
1 No. 18 to 24 large brush
1 No. 8 or 10 fine round brush

## Other Materials

1 graphite stick, 1 sheet of gray paper, fabric scissors

This picture is made in the same way as Sleeping Cat, except that you paint the background of the drawing white. As the final step, we also painted a narrow white border around the drawing that overlaps the fabric.

# CHERRY BLOSSOMS

Total time to complete: approximately 2 days

Technique: freehand

Layout Diagram: Template H – 3

Finished art shown on page 82

## Main Materials

- 3 natural canvases on 7⅞" x 31½" (20 x 80 cm) stretcher frames
- 1 jar of acrylic binder
- Acrylic paints: yellow earth, white, vermilion, and burnt umber
- 1 small cup of strong black coffee
- 1 No. 18 to 28 large brush
- 2 No. 8 or 10 small round brushes

## Other Materials

1 set of measuring spoons, 1 large cup (or 1 bowl)

**1**

**2**

**3**

1 Background: 20 minutes / Drying Time: 2 hours
Stand the canvases upright, side by side. Mix together the coffee, white paint, and two tablespoons of acrylic binder in a large cup or a bowl. Paint this mixture onto the canvases with the large brush, using irregular vertical brushstrokes to give a patina effect. Let dry.

2 Painting: 30 minutes / Drying Time: 1 hour
Prepare the color for the tree branches by mixing together white, yellow earth, and burnt umber paints. Position the canvases side by side and then paint the branches freehand with the small brush using very little water. You can use Layout Diagram 3 of Template H to guide you, or follow your own design. Let dry.

3 Detail Painting: 10 minutes / Drying Time: 1 hour
When the branch paint is dry, use a clean small brush and vermilion paint to add the red dots to the branches. You can also add some smaller branch details, if desired. Let dry.

# APPAREL ART

Total time to complete: approximately 2 days
Technique: fabric collage
Pattern: Template I – 1

Finished art shown on page 83

## Main Materials

- 1 white canvas on 18⅛" x 24" (46 x 61 cm) stretcher frame
- 1 jar of acrylic binder
- 1 No. 24 to 40 large brush
- 4 lengths of fabric in different colors and prints

## Other Materials

1 lead pencil, 1 graphite stick, 1 stick of white chalk, black tissue paper (or butcher paper or newspaper), fabric scissors

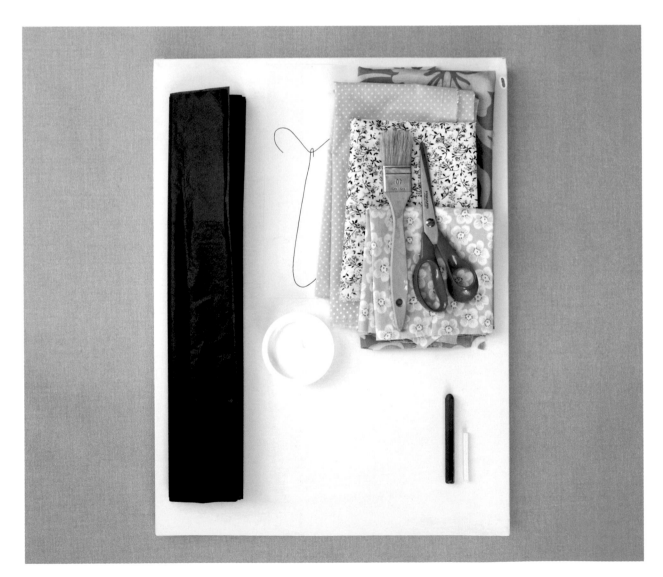

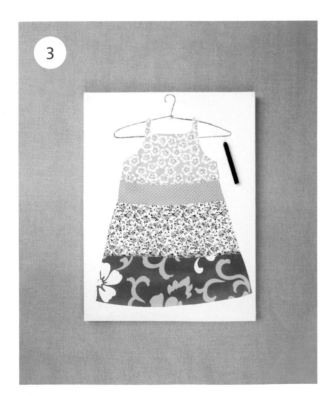

1 Pattern: 15 minutes / Cutting: 15 minutes
Using the white chalk, draw a small pattern for a dress freehand on the tissue paper and cut the pattern into four sections. Place each section of the pattern on your chosen piece of fabric and trace around it with the lead pencil. Cut out all the pieces of the pattern.

2 Collage: 10 minutes / Drying Time: 1 hour
Arrange all the fabric pieces of the dress on the canvas, leaving enough space at the top for the hanger. When you have the arrangement you like, coat each dress piece with acrylic binder using the large brush, placing the pieces of fabric in position on the canvas as you go. Then brush acrylic binder over the entire canvas, smoothing out the fabric with the brush or with the heels of your hands, if necessary (the acrylic binder washes off with water). Let dry.

3 Drawing: 10 minutes / Drying Time: 1 hour
When the acrylic binder is dry, draw a stylized hanger on the canvas with the graphite stick, following Pattern 1 of Template I.

# PYRAMID SCHEME

Total time to complete: approximately a half day
Technique: hand-printing

Finished art shown on page 84

## Main Materials

- 2 white canvases on 11⅞" x 23⅝" (30 x 60 cm) stretcher frames
- 1 white canvas on 23⅝" x 23⅝" (60 x 60 cm) stretcher frame
- 1 No. 14 to 24 large brush
- 1 No. 8 or 10 small flat brush
- Acrylic paints: indigo and white
- 1 tube of acrylic binder
- 1 potato

## Other Materials

1 craft knife (or 1 small kitchen knife)

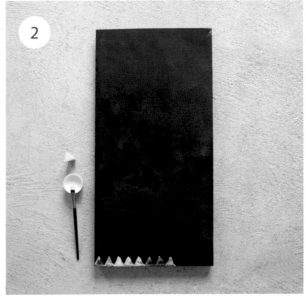

1 Hand-Stamp: 5 minutes
Using the craft knife or a small kitchen knife, cut a triangle out of a peeled potato to make a hand-stamp, with a "handle" to hold on to.

2 Painting: 30 minutes / Drying Time: 1 hour
Paint the background of each canvas with indigo paint and the large brush. Dilute the paint a little with acrylic binder so that the paint adheres better to the canvas. Let dry. To make the first row of triangles, apply a little paint to the stamp with the small brush to obtain an even result. For a stronger color effect, dip the stamp directly into the paint and apply it to the canvas.

3 Painting: 1 hour / Drying Time: 1 hour
Continue to add rows of triangles to the canvas one above the other, alternating the density of the white paint. For a true pyramid effect, each white triangle should have a corresponding inverted blue triangle above it; follow the pattern as shown.

★ FINAL TIP
Don't try to make the background paint totally uniform. You'll find that slight color variations will enliven the design and break up the overall geometric effect.

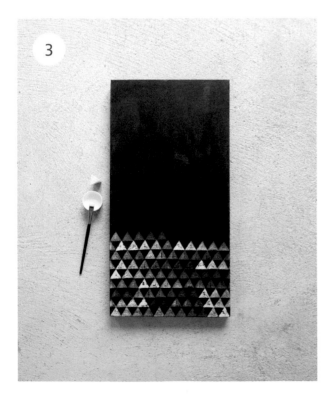

# LITTLE BLUE HOUSE

Total time to complete: approximately 2 days
Technique: coating / tracing
Pattern: Template I – 2

Finished art shown on page 85

## Main Materials

- 1 white canvas on 31½" x 47¼" (80 x 120 cm) stretcher frame
- 1 jar of acrylic pumice medium
- 1 palette knife
- Acrylic paints: white, ultramarine blue, buff titanium/warm white, black, and burnt umber
- 1 No. 18 to 24 large brush
- 1 No. 8 or 10 small flat brush

## Other Materials

1 sheet of paper, 1 lead pencil, 1 stick of white chalk, 1 long graduated ruler, scissors, 1 craft knife

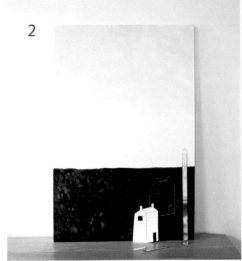

1 Earth: 15 minutes / Drying Time: overnight
With the palette knife, coat the bottom one-third of the canvas with acrylic pumice medium, applying small dabs of the mortar side by side. To achieve gray accents in different shades, add small, random dabs of black, ultramarine blue, and burnt umber paints with the small brush.

2 Sky: 10 minutes / Drying Time: 1 hour
Paint the sky with the large brush, starting at the top of the canvas and using regular horizontal and vertical brushstrokes across the canvas. Keep the canvas flat on your work surface so that the paint does not run. To achieve a graduated wash effect in the sky, mix a touch of white paint with the aquamarine blue and gradually add more white paint and water as you work down the canvas. Let dry.

3 Drawing: 10 minutes / Painting: 10 minutes
Drying Time: 1 hour
Make a tracing of Pattern 2 of Template I on the white paper and cut out the house with the scissors. Carefully cut out the window and door using the craft knife. Place the house in position on the canvas and draw around the outline with the chalk. Using a clean small brush, paint the front of the house with white paint and the roof and sides with buff titanium/warm white. The roof lines and the corner of the house should be left visible.

# CHAPTER 5 YOUTHFUL SPACES

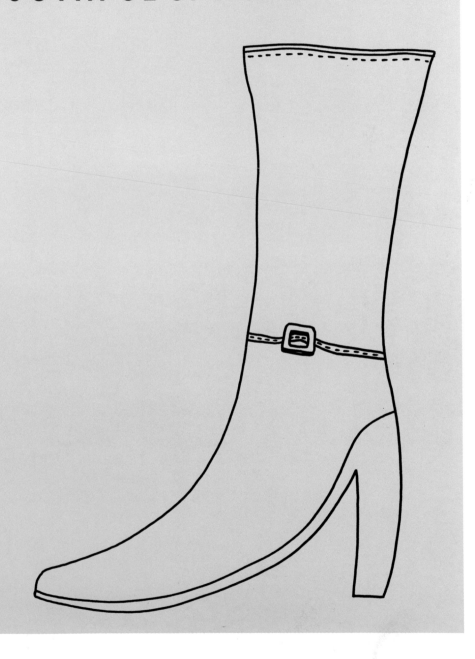

Ella

## THE FACES OF ELLA
Instructions on pages 108 and 109

# SHOES & BOOTS
Instructions on pages 110 to 113

VIBRANT VILLAGE
Instructions on pages 114 and 115

SPANISH TILE
Instructions in pages 116 and 117

# THE FACES OF ELLA

Total time to complete: approximately 1 day

Techniques: collage / freehand

Finished art shown on page 104

## Other Materials

1 lead pencil, 1 long graduated ruler, 1 craft knife

## Main Materials

- 1 white canvas on 15¾" x 15¾" (40 x 40 cm) stretcher frame
- 1 jar of acrylic binder
- Tubes of acrylic paint: Mars black, titanium white, cadmium red, cadmium green, primary yellow, Naples yellow, and cobalt blue
- 1 No. 40 large brush
- 1 fine brush
- Photocopies of the photographs and a name printed in black-and-white

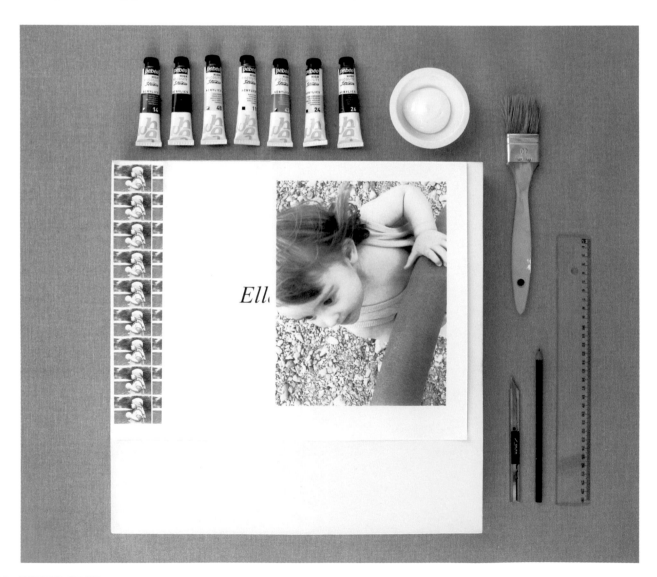

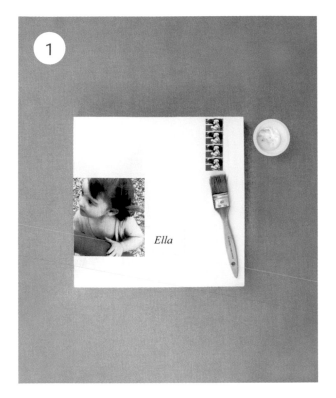

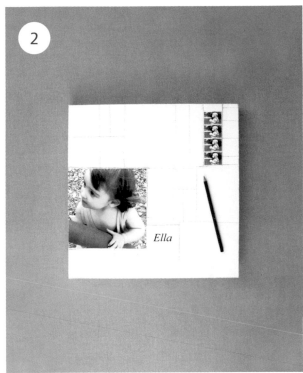

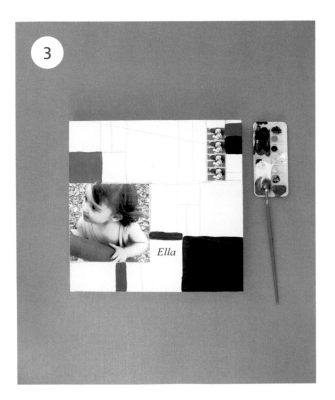

1 Collage: 5 minutes / Drying Time: 1 hour
Apply acrylic binder to the canvas with the large brush and then arrange the photocopies in your desired pattern on the canvas. Using a clean large brush, apply acrylic binder over the photocopies. In this step the acrylic binder acts as a glue, so it shouldn't be diluted. Let dry.

2 Drawing: 10 minutes
Draw rectangles in different sizes on the canvas with the lead pencil.

3 Painting: 20 minutes / Drying Time: 1 hour
With the fine brush and using very little water, paint the rectangles in different colors, as desired. Work in color groups, mixing the paints with white and black and other combinations for different shades at the same time, and let the paint dry between each group. Start with red, then green and yellow, and finally white and blue. Let dry.

# SHOES & BOOTS

Total time to complete: approximately 1 day
Techniques: stenciling / tracing
Patterns: Template J

Finished art shown on page 105

## Other Materials

1 sheet of tracing paper, 1 lead pencil, 1 stick of red chalk, scissors, 1 craft knife

## Main Materials

- 1 white canvas on 11⅞" x 15¾" (30 x 40 cm) stretcher frame
- Acrylic paints: light blue (white + ultramarine blue), pink, and black
- 1 No. 18 to 24 large brush
- 1 No. 8 or 10 small brush
- 1 fine brush
- 1 sheet of Frisket adhesive paper film, 11⅞" x 15¾" (30 x 40 cm)

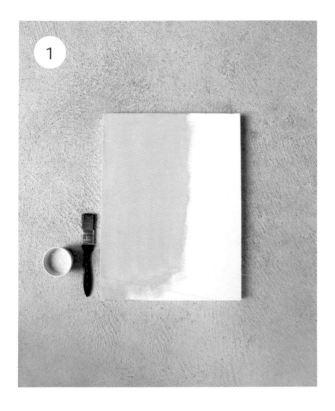

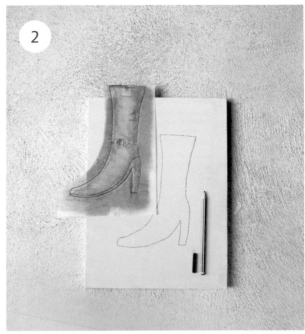

1 Background: 30 minutes / Drying Time: 1 hour
Mix white and blue paints to make light blue, then paint the canvas with the large brush, crossing your brushstrokes horizontally and vertically for an even coat. Moisten the brush periodically using very little water and blot it before adding paint. Let dry.

2 Tracing: 5 minutes / Transfer: 10 minutes
Using the lead pencil, trace the boot pattern of Template J onto a sheet of tracing paper, including the buckle and the sole. Cut out the tracing so that you can easily position it on the canvas. Cover the back of the tracing paper with red chalk and place the paper on the canvas, chalk side down, with the motif in the center. Retrace the outline of the boot with the pencil, pressing firmly so that the red chalk is transferred to the canvas. Remove the tracing paper and put it to one side. Blow off any loose chalk.

3 Stenciling: 10 minutes
Cover the canvas with a sheet of Frisket adhesive film, smoothing out any creases or bubbles. Using the craft knife, carefully cut around the outline of the boot and remove the cut-out shape, leaving the boot stencil on the canvas.

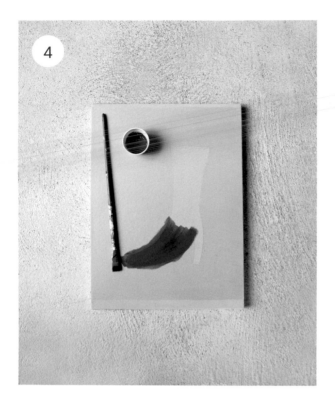

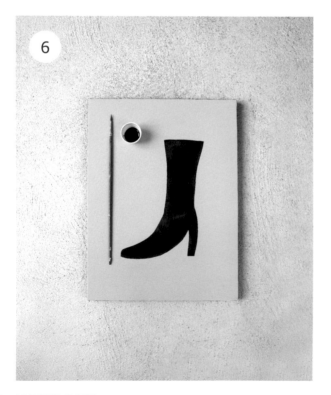

4 Painting: 15 minutes / Drying Time: 1 hour
  Paint the boot with pink using the small brush and undiluted paint (so that it doesn't run), crossing your brushstrokes evenly. Let the picture dry well before removing the Frisket adhesive film.

5 Tracing: 5 minutes
  Reposition the chalk-covered tracing exactly over the boot shape with the chalk side down. With the pencil, trace over the buckle and the sole again to transfer these details onto the canvas in red chalk. Remove the stencil and blow off any loose chalk on the canvas.

6 Details: 10 minutes / Drying Time: 10 minutes
  With the fine brush, paint the details of the buckle and sole using black paint, then the outline of the top of the boot. If you don't want to use paint, you can use a lead pencil or graphite stick instead.

# THE COMPLETE COLLECTION

Total time to complete: approximately 1 day
Techniques: stenciling / tracing
Patterns: Template J

## Main Materials

- 1 white canvas on 11⅞" x 15¾" (30 x 40 cm) stretcher frame
- Acrylic paints: pink and gold
- 1 No. 8 or 10 small brush
- 1 fine brush, or 1 lead pencil
- 1 sheet of Frisket adhesive paper film, 11⅞" x 15¾" (30 x 40 cm)

## Other Materials

1 sheet of tracing paper, 1 lead pencil, 1 stick of red chalk, scissors, 1 craft knife

Make The Complete Collection in the same way as you made the Shoes & Boots painting, using the other shoe and boot patterns of Template J. We left the background unpainted, but the final background is up to you. You can either paint in the small details with the fine brush or draw them in with a lead pencil.

# VIBRANT VILLAGE

Total time to complete: approximately 1 day
Techniques: tracing / freehand
Patterns: Templates K and L

Finished art shown on page 106

## Other Materials

5 sheets of white paper, 1 lead pencil, scissors

## Main Materials

- 1 white canvas on 31½" x 39⅜" (80 x 100 cm) stretcher frame
- Acrylic paints: titanium beige, white, primary yellow, medium cadmium yellow, dark cadmium yellow, vermilion, magenta, and pink
- 1 No. 18 to 28 large brush
- 1 No. 8 to 10 small brush

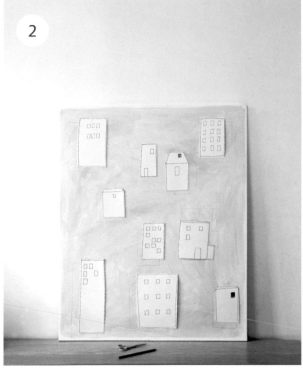

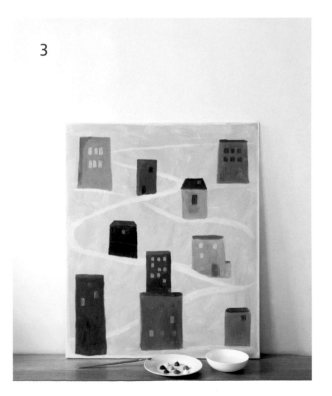

1 Background: 20 minutes / Drying Time: 1 hour
Paint the background in titanium beige with the large brush. Wet the brush well to dilute the paint and use loose brushstrokes so that the canvas has an uneven paint layer. Let dry thoroughly.

2 Tracing and Cutting: 30 minutes
Trace the patterns on Templates K and L onto the sheets of paper using the lead pencil. Cut out the shapes and trace their outlines on the canvas with the pencil.

3 Painting: 30 minutes / Drying Time: 1 hour
With the small brush, paint the houses, roofs, and windows in different shades of orange and ochre by mixing together the acrylic paint colors. Use very little water on the brush. Then use a clean small brush to paint a white path that weaves between the houses. Let dry.

# SPANISH TILE

Total time to complete: approximately 2 days
Techniques: coating / freehand
Layout Diagram: Template I - 3

Finished art shown on page 107

## Other Materials

1 long graduated ruler

## Main Materials

- 1 white canvas on 35½" x 23⅝" (90 x 60 cm) stretcher frame
- 1 jar of modeling paste
- 1 palette knife
- Acrylic paints: orange, dark cadmium yellow, fluorescent orange, yellow earth, and white
- 1 No. 8 to 10 small round brush
- 1 fine brush

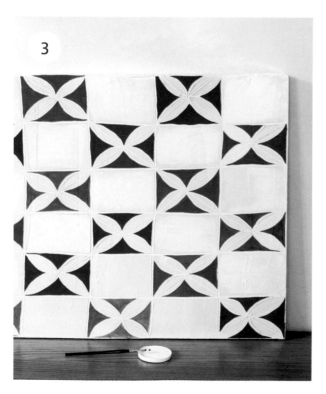

1 Background: 10 minutes / Drawing: 10 minutes
With the palette knife, apply modeling paste generously all over the canvas to create a textured finish. While the modeling paste is still wet, use the ruler and the tip of the handle of the fine brush to draw a checkerboard of boxes measuring 4" x 5⅞" (10 x 15 cm) on the canvas.

2 Drawing: 10 minutes / Drying Time: overnight
Once you have finished the checkerboard, continue using the tip of the brush handle to draw an X in every other rectangle, alternating the boxes in each row. Then draw a flower motif over the X following Layout Diagram 3 of Template I. Let the modeling paste dry overnight.

3 Painting: 20 minutes / Drying Time: 10 minutes
Using the small brush with very little water, paint the flower backgrounds in shades of orange. Use the fine brush for detailed areas. Then paint the empty boxes white using the small brush.

# CHAPTER 6

# OFFICE DÉCOR

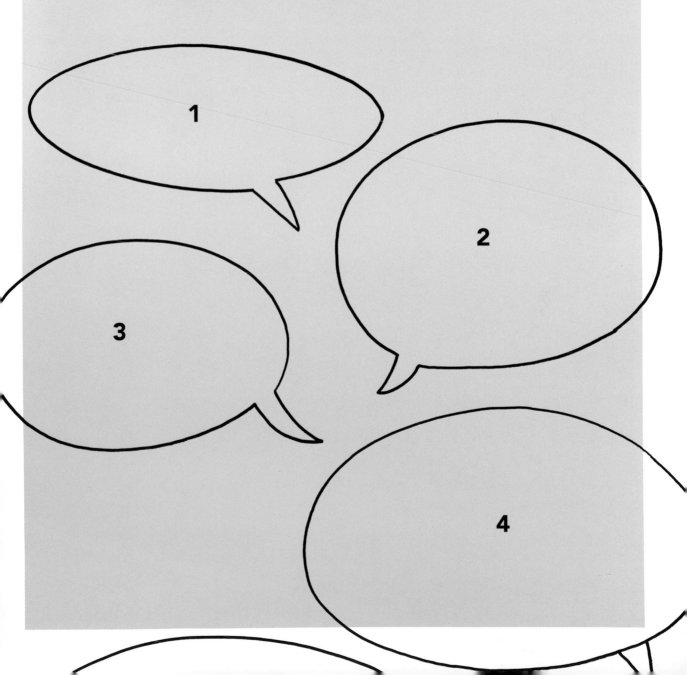

ORANGE BLOSSOMS
Instructions on pages 126 to 129

# PLAYING WITH DOTS
Instructions on pages 132 and 133

# LEAFY TREE
Instructions on pages 134 to 137

STRIPED SERIES
Instructions on pages 140 to 143

# ORANGE BLOSSOMS

Total time to complete: approximately a half day
Techniques: painting / tracing
Pattern: Template M

Finished art shown on page 120

## Main Materials

- 1 white canvas on 18⅛" x 21⅝" (46 x 55 cm) stretcher frame
- Acrylic paints: turquoise blue and white
- 1 No. 18 to 24 large brush
- 1 fine brush
- 3 medium-point paint markers: dark orange, orange, and white

## Other Materials

1 sheet of tracing paper (18⅛" x 21⅝"/46 x 55 cm), 1 lead pencil, 1 stick of red chalk

**1**

**2**

**3**

1 Background: 15 minutes / Drying Time: 1 hour
  With the large brush, paint an even turquoise
  blue background on the canvas, leaving a narrow,
  irregular strip unpainted all around the edge. Cross
  your brushstrokes horizontally and vertically for an
  even coat. Moisten the brush using very little water
  periodically and blot it before adding more paint.
  Let dry.

2 Tracing: 30 minutes
  With the lead pencil, trace the patterns of Template
  M onto a large sheet of tracing paper.

3 Transfer: 10 minutes
  Apply a generous layer of red chalk onto the back
  of the tracing paper. Place the tracing paper on
  the canvas, chalk side down, and then retrace the
  outlines of the design with the pencil so that the red
  chalk is transferred to the canvas in your desired pattern. Blow off any loose chalk.

**4 Color Drawing: 30 minutes**

Draw over the stems and the outlines of the leaves with the white marker. Fill in the inner petals of the flowers with the orange marker and the outer petals with the dark orange marker.

**5 Painting: 30 minutes**

Use the white paint and the fine brush to fill in the insides of the leaves, using very little water. Let dry.

## ★ FINAL TIP

If you feel secure enough using the fine brush and the white paint, you can paint the stems and flower details instead of using the white marker.

# IN THE ROUND

Total time to complete: approximately 2 days
Techniques: stenciling / freehand
Layout Diagram: Template N

Finished art shown on page 121

## Main Materials

- 3 white canvases on 23⅝" x 23⅝" (60 x 60 cm) 3-D stretcher frames
- Acrylic paints: turquoise blue, indigo, iridescent copper, and iridescent silver
- 1 No. 18 to 24 large brush
- 1 No. 10 to 18 medium brush

## Other Materials

1 sheet of white paper, 1 lead pencil, scissors, compass

**1**

**2**

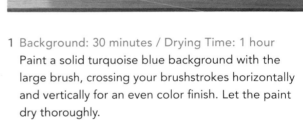

1 Background: 30 minutes / Drying Time: 1 hour
Paint a solid turquoise blue background with the large brush, crossing your brushstrokes horizontally and vertically for an even color finish. Let the paint dry thoroughly.

2 Drawing: 10 minutes
Draw a circle on a sheet of paper with the compass and cut it out. Using this circle as a pattern template, draw circles and semicircles on the canvas with the lead pencil. The Layout Diagrams of Template N give you some ideas of how to position them.

**3**

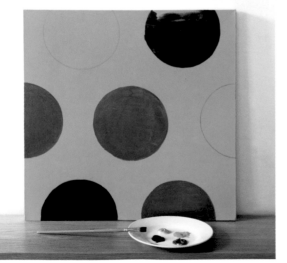

3 Painting: 1 hour
Paint the circles in iridescent copper, indigo, and iridescent silver with the medium brush, using very little water. Apply a second coat of paint if necessary. Let dry.

## ★ FINAL TIP

For the second canvas, paint alternating small turquoise blue and copper circles on a silver background. For the third painting, paint an indigo background, then turquoise blue circles and just one copper circle. Have the circles almost touch so that they cover most of the canvas.

# PLAYING WITH DOTS

Total time to complete: approximately 2 days

Techniques: coating / freehand

Finished art shown on page 122

## Main Materials

- 1 white canvas on 18⅛" x 24" (46 x 61 cm) stretcher frame
- 1 jar of gesso paste
- 1 palette knife
- Acrylic paints: iridescent silver, dark gray, light gray, and white
- 1 No. 18 to 24 large brush
- 1 No. 8 or 10 small brush

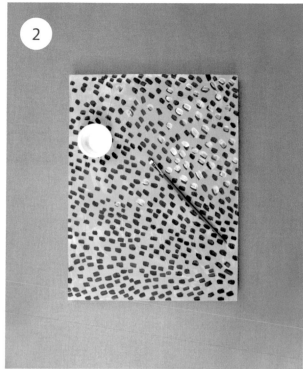

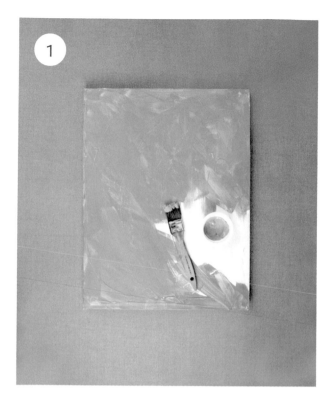

1 Background: 15 minutes / Drying Time: overnight
Painting: 15 minutes

Apply a generous coating of gesso paste to the canvas, spreading it vertically and horizontally over the entire surface with the palette knife. Let dry overnight. When totally dry, paint the background light gray with the large brush, moistening the brush periodically using very little water and blotting before you add more paint. Let dry.

2 Painting: 15 minutes / Drying Time: 1 hour

With the small brush, apply small dabs of dark gray paint all over the canvas for a stippled effect. Don't moisten the brush very much. When the dark gray stippled layer is dry, go over the dots with white paint, again in stippled dabs, slightly off center to the gray dots below. Add a few isolated white dots here and there, if you desire.

3 Painting: 10 minutes / Drying Time: 1 hour

When the white stippling is dry, paint some stippled silver dabs over them here and there, again slightly off center, to create a shadow effect. Let dry.

# LEAFY TREE

Total time to complete: approximately 2 days
Techniques: coating / freehand
Pattern: Template N – 1

Finished art shown on page 123

## Main Materials

- 1 natural canvas on 23⅝" x 23⅝" (60 x 60 cm) 3-D stretcher frame
- 1 jar of gesso paste
- Acrylic paints: white, primary yellow, Hooker's green, black, cadmium green, yellow earth, chrome green
- 2 No. 18 to 24 large brushes
- 1 No. 8 or 10 small brush

## Other Materials

1 piece of white Bristol board, 1 sheet of tracing paper, 1 lead pencil, 1 craft knife

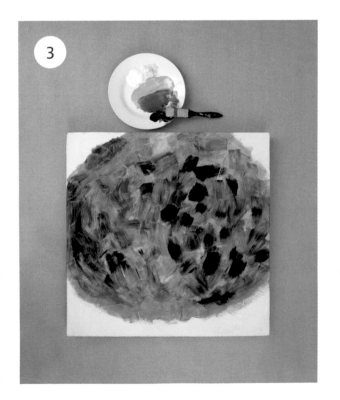

1 Background: 15 minutes / Drying Time: overnight
Coat the canvas with gesso paste to give it a textured finish, applying the paste with the large brush. Start at the bottom right corner and work to the top, crossing your brushstrokes on the canvas. Let dry overnight.

2 Background: 10 minutes / Drying Time: 1 hour
Mix together white and primary yellow paints. With the large brush, apply the mixture to the canvas in small dabs and use short brushstrokes to cover the canvas evenly. Moisten the brush periodically using very little water and blot before adding paint. Let dry.

3 Foliage: 20 minutes / Drying Time: 1 hour
Paint the leaves with a clean large brush, using overlapping dabs of paint in cadmium green, Hooker's green, chrome green, and white. Use the colors both pure and mixed, and let the brushstrokes remain visible. Let dry.

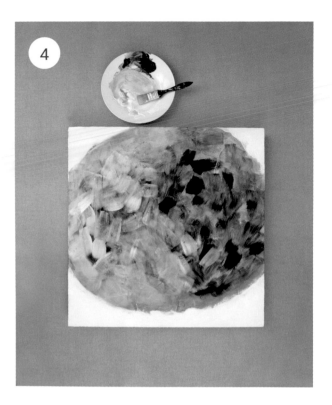

**4** Foliage: 20 minutes / Drying Time: 1 hour

When the green foliage is dry, add some touches of mixed white and yellow earth paints with the large brush. Let dry. Paint the corners of the canvas white using a clean large brush so that the rounded shape of the tree stands out.

**5** Tree Trunk: 30 minutes / Drying Time: 1 hour

Trace Pattern 1 of Template N onto the piece of Bristol board. Cut out the trunk using the craft knife, position the pattern on the canvas, and then trace it with the lead pencil. Mix together Hooker's green and black paints and paint the tree trunk and its branches using the small brush. Let dry.

## ★ FINAL TIP

Try to have the tree trunk and branches blend into the leaves by tapering their edges where they meet. You can also go back and paint some overlapping foliage once the trunk is dry.

# SPEECH BUBBLES

Total time to complete: approximately 1 day
Techniques: drawing / freehand
Pattern: Template O

Finished art shown on page 124

## Other Materials

2 sheets of white paper, 1 lead pencil, 1 colored pencil
or felt-tip marker, scissors

## Main Materials

- 1 white canvas on 11⅞" x 23⅝" (30 x 60 cm)
  stretcher frame
- Tubes of acrylic paint: black, white, cadmium orange,
  cadmium red, cadmium green, and cobalt blue
- 1 No. 18 to 28 large brush
- 1 No. 10 to 18 medium brush
- 1 fine brush

**1**

**2**

**3**

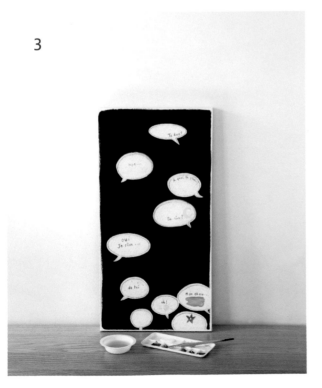

**1** Background: 30 minutes / Drying Time: 1 hour
Paint the canvas black using the large brush, leaving a small white border all around the edge. Use very little water on the brush and cross your brushstrokes so the canvas is covered evenly.

**2** Drawing: 20 minutes / Painting: 20 minutes
Drying Time: 1 hour
Copy Patterns 1 to 10 of Template O onto a sheet of paper using the lead pencil and cut them out. Arrange them on the canvas in your desired configuration and then trace them with the colored pencil or marker. Paint the insides of the speech bubbles white using the medium brush and very little water. Apply a second layer of paint, if necessary, to achieve a solid coat.

**3** Pencil: 20 minutes / Painting: 20 minutes
Drying Time: 1 hour
Write your choice of words and phrases in pencil or marker inside the speech bubbles. Using the fine brush and your choice of paint colors, paint whimsical little motifs freehand inside the bubbles.

# STRIPED SERIES

Total time to complete: approximately 2 days

Techniques: masking

Finished art shown on page 125

## Main Materials

- 8 white canvases on 11⅞" x 11⅞" (30 x 30 cm) 3-D stretcher frames
- Acrylic paints: bright yellow, buff titanium/warm white, dark cadmium yellow, crimson, white, and burnt umber
- 1 No. 10 to 18 medium brush

## Other Materials

1 short graduated ruler, 1 lead pencil, masking tape (1⅛"/3 cm wide), scissors

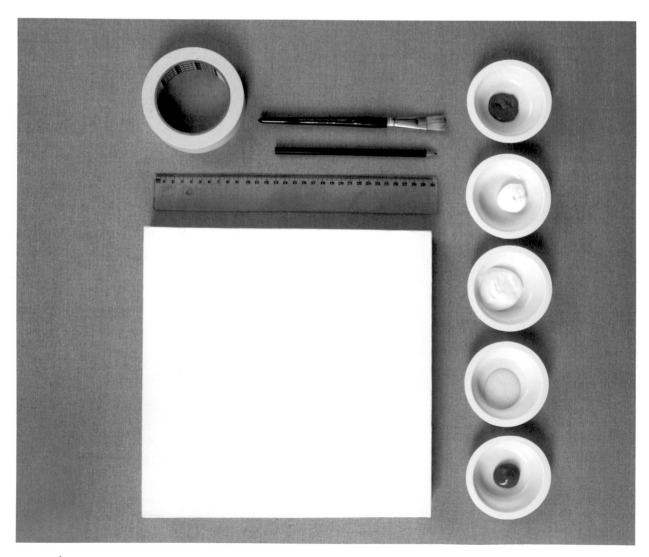

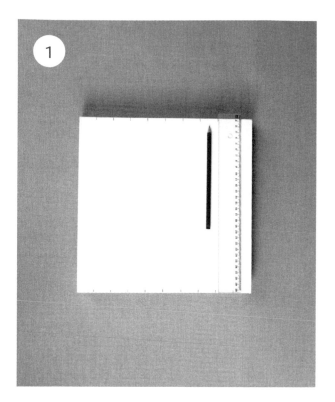

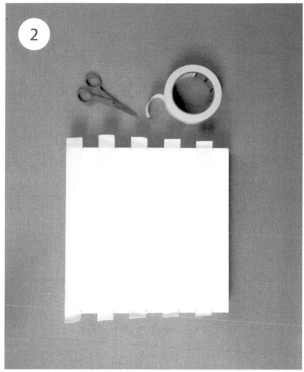

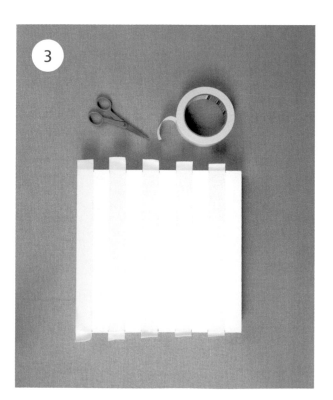

1 Marking: 10 minutes

Use the graduated ruler and a lead pencil to mark the top and bottom of one of the canvases every 1⅛" (3 cm).

2 Taping: 10 minutes

Using your pencil marks as a guide, apply strips of masking tape to the canvas at the 1⅛" (3 cm) intervals, as shown.

3 Painting: 20 minutes / Drying Time: 1 hour

Paint the first three stripes and the last stripe in bright yellow with the medium brush. Barely moisten the brush so that the paint doesn't run beneath the masking tape. Don't be afraid to paint over the top of the masking tape—this will help you get a clean, sharp edge to the stripes.

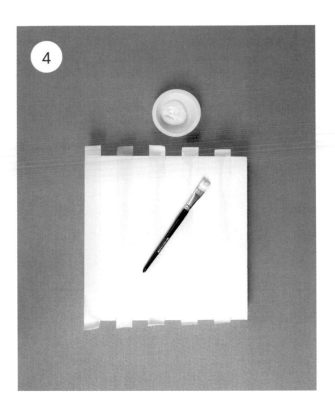

**4** Painting: 5 minutes / Drying Time: 1 hour
Paint the remaining stripe the same way with buff titanium paint. Let dry.

**5** Remove Tape: 10 minutes
Once the paint is completely dry, carefully remove the tape.

**6 to 9** Other paintings in this series
Make the next three paintings in the same manner, but with pink stripes (mix together crimson and white), gray stripes (mix together crimson, white, and burnt umber), and dark cadmium yellow stripes. Line up the contrasting stripes in whatever pattern you prefer.

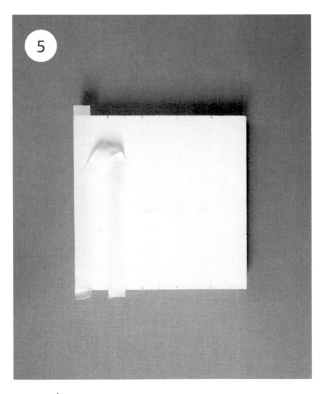

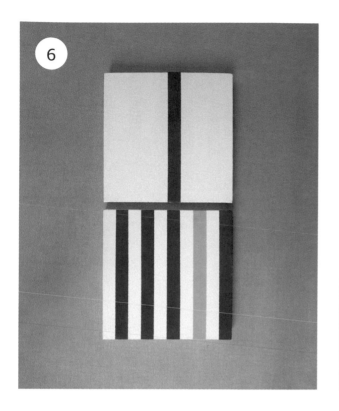

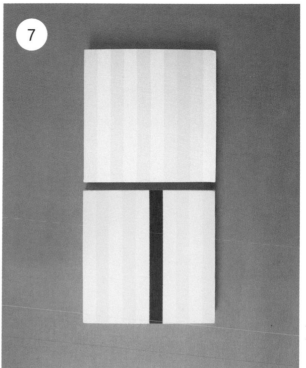

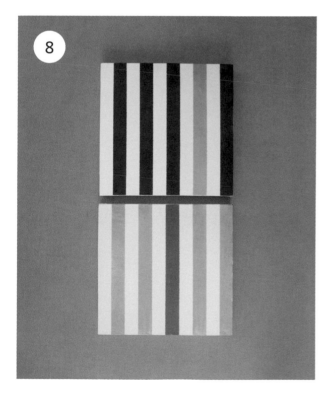

# resources

# acknowledgments

You can find many of the supplies needed for the projects in this book through the following online retailers or at your local arts and crafts supply store:

**Golden**
www.goldenpaints.com

**Jo-Ann**
www.joann.com

**Liquitex**
www.liquitex.com

**Michael's**
www.michaels.com

**Pearl Paint**
www.pearlpaint.com

**Pébéo**
www.pebeo.com/us

**Utrecht Art Supply**
www.utrechtart.com

# index

Sophie Glasser, Hiroko Mori, Marie François, Rose Marie Di Domenico, Pascale Caron, Colin Richard, Ella, Sémélé, Catherine Hardy and Brieuc Segalen, Gérard and Claude Gavarry, Colette and Alain Richard, Xavier Lang, Bruno Verrier, Manu, Fleur, Alice, and Gwen.

With thanks to Pébéo and to Patricia Chaveau, who supplied all the paints, brushes, and other small items, as well as all the canvases used to create the artwork in this book.

Text copyright © 2010 by Lola Gavarry
Photography copyright © 2010 by Hiroko Mori
Translation from French by Moura MacDonagh

Published in the United States by Watson-Guptill Publications, an imprint of the Crown Publishing Group, a division of Random House, Inc., New York.
www.crownpublishing.com
www.watsonguptill.com

First published in France by Marabout (Hachette Livre) in 2008.

WATSON-GUPTILL is a registered trademark and the WG and Horse designs are trademarks of Random House, Inc.

Library of Congress Cataloging-in-Publication Data

Gavarry, Lola.
  [Home deco des tableaux a peindre. English]
  DIY art at home : 28 simple projects for chic décor on the cheap : with 15 full-size, tear-out templates / Lola Gavarry ; photography by Hiroko Mori.
       p. cm.
  ISBN 978-0-8230-3334-8 (pbk. : alk. paper)
  1.  Painting—Technique. 2.  Decoration and ornament.
I. Title.
  TT385.G38913 2010
  745.7'23—dc22
                                        2009047261

Printed in China
Design by Vera Thamsir Fong

10 9 8 7 6 5 4 3 2 1

First Edition